Writing Handbook

Teacher's Guide

GRADE
4

Printed in the U.S.A.

ISBN: 978-0-547-86457-0

22 23 24 25   0982   24 23 22 21 20 19 18

4500695866   F G

Houghton Mifflin Harcourt

Contents

Writing Strategies

WRITING MODELS AND FORMS (continued)

How to Use This Book

The *Writing Handbook* was designed to complement the writing instruction in your reading program as well as meet all academic standards for writing. It consists of two components: a handbook for students that they can refer to as a resource as well as practice writing in throughout the year, and a Teacher's Guide that supports instruction by providing minilessons for every handbook topic.

Components

Two easy-to-use components make up the *Writing Handbook* program:

- For Grades 2–6, a 160-page partially consumable student handbook with 30 writing topics that correlate to your reading program's lessons.

  The first section of each grade-level handbook includes writing models along with interactive practice to scaffold or reinforce students' understanding of opinion, informational/explanatory, and narrative writing. As students practice writing, they build additional examples of forms to refer to throughout the year as well as develop a deeper understanding of each form's structure.

  The second section of the handbook is a resource tool that students can refer to whenever they write. Topics range from writing strategies to how to use technology to do research.

- For Grade 1, a 96-page partially consumable student handbook also includes 30 correlated handbook topics followed by a resource section on writing strategies, such as the writing process and writing traits.

- For Grades K–6, a Teacher's Guide with 60 minilessons for section 1 (two minilessons for each section 1 student handbook topic) plus one minilesson, as needed, for each remaining page of the resource handbook. The Kindergarten Teacher's Guide includes an abundance of copying masters.

Minilessons

Minilessons are short, focused lessons on specific topics. For each minilesson, you will demonstrate an aspect of writing before students try their own hand. In this Teacher's Guide, minilessons are provided for each topic in the handbook. In the first section are two minilessons for each topic. Each of these minilessons consists of the following parts:

- Topic title
- Tab with section name
- Minilesson number and title
- Objective and guiding question
- Easy-to-follow instruction in an *I Do*, *We Do*, and *You Do* format
- Modeled, collaborative, and independent writing
- Conference and evaluation information

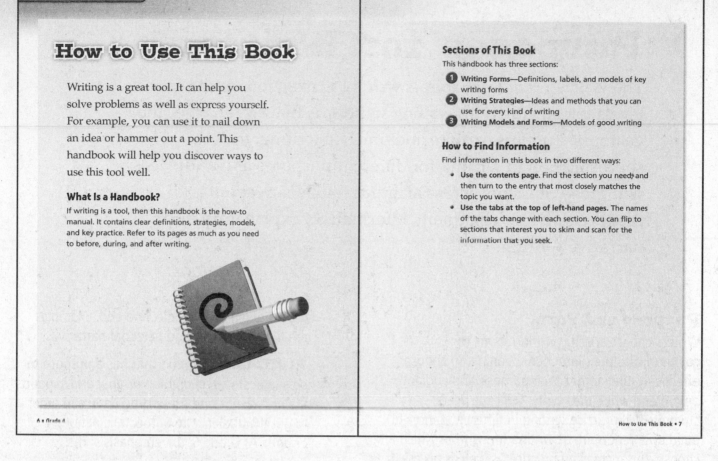

How to Use This Book

Writing is a great tool. It can help you solve problems as well as express yourself. For example, you can use it to nail down an idea or hammer out a point. This handbook will help you discover ways to use this tool well.

What Is a Handbook?

If writing is a tool, then this handbook is the how-to manual. It contains clear definitions, strategies, models, and key practice. Refer to its pages as much as you need to before, during, and after writing.

Sections of This Book

This handbook has three sections:

1. **Writing Forms**—Definitions, labels, and models of key writing forms
2. **Writing Strategies**—Ideas and methods that you can use for every kind of writing
3. **Writing Models and Forms**—Models of good writing

How to Find Information

Find information in this book in two different ways:

- **Use the contents page.** Find the section you need, and then turn to the entry that most closely matches the topic you want.
- **Use the tabs at the top of left-hand pages.** The names of the tabs change with each section. You can flip to sections that interest you to skim and scan for the information that you seek.

- Technology references
- Reduced facsimiles of student handbook pages
- Tips for corrective feedback
- A feature that further explores the lesson's writing trait

Each writing minilesson has been correlated to your reading program's writing lessons so that all minilessons and corresponding writing handbook pages within this section are used at least once during the school year. Additional minilessons are provided throughout the Teacher's Guide and correlate to each remaining page in the handbook. Use these minilessons, as needed, to clarify concepts for students and provide additional support.

Student-Page Walk-Through

Have students turn to and read pages 6 and 7 in their books. Explain to them that their handbook is a tool that they can use whenever they write. It can help them find information quickly about any writing question they have, and they can use it to help them during writing. Guide students to find

each of these parts in their handbooks:

- Table of contents
- Introductory pages, including overviews of the writing process and the writing traits
- Writing form pages, each with a section tab, title, definition, and helpful bulleted points, followed by a clear example of the writing model as well as a write-in activity page
- Additional reference pages on topics ranging from writing strategies to revising to using technology, as well as more examples of writing models they may need or want to refer to during the year for projects and other assignments
- An index. Remind students that the table of contents is in order of presentation while the index is ordered alphabetically.

Purposes for Writing

The *Writing Handbook* spirals writing instruction up the grade levels to coincide with writing standards that spiral. Over the years, as students explore and practice writing, their sophistication in writing for different purposes and audiences will grow. Students across all grades will learn about and practice opinion/argument, informative/explanatory, and narrative writing.

Purpose and Form

Writers choose specific writing forms to communicate their intended meaning. To choose effectively, they target their purpose and audience before and while they write. Over the years, students will practice writing in different genres to build up a repertoire of writing forms from which to choose. This increasing practice as well as access to information about writing will help students feel more comfortable about writing and, hopefully, enjoy doing it.

In this handbook, the writing forms and models presented coincide primarily with the purposes expressed through the academic standards. These are to inform, to explain, to narrate, and to persuade. There are other purposes for writing as well, but these four are emphasized to best prepare students for college and career readiness.

TO INFORM The purpose for writing to inform is to share facts and other information. Informational texts such as reports make statements that are supported by facts and truthful evidence.

TO EXPLAIN The purpose for writing to explain is to tell *what, how,* and *why* about a topic. An example is to explain in writing how to do or make something.

TO NARRATE The purpose of writing to narrate is to tell a story. The story can be made up or truthful. Most forms of narrative writing have a beginning, middle, and end. Examples are fictional stories and personal narratives.

TO PERSUADE Writing that has a purpose to persuade states an opinion or goal and supports it with reasons and supporting details in order to get the audience to agree, take action, or both. At Grade 6, the emphasis shifts to argument.

Over the years, as their writing grows more sophisticated, students may find that their purpose for writing is a hybrid of two or more purposes. An example would be literary nonfiction that includes elements of storytelling although it may be written primarily to inform and explain. Another example would be historical fiction that tells a story but relates events accurately in order to inform the reader as well.

Success in School and Life

Students and adults are often judged by how well they can communicate. Students are encouraged to learn to write effectively to be successful in their studies. In particular, by the upper grades, they need to master the basic essay format that includes

- An introductory paragraph that identifies the topic or statement of purpose.

- Supporting paragraphs that provide related details and examples.

Purposes for Writing

When you write, one of the first things you should do is think about your purpose. Your **purpose** is your main reason for writing. There are many purposes for writing, but four of the main ones are to inform, to explain, to narrate, or to persuade.

● **To Inform**

To inform is to give or share information. This means writing and sharing facts and details. Some examples of writing that to inform include reports, informational essays, and instructions.

● **To Explain**

To explain means to tell more about a topic by telling what, why, and how. Some kinds of writing that explain are instructions, how-to paragraphs, and explanations.

● **To Narrate**

To narrate means to tell a story, whether that story is true or made up. Some examples of narrative writing include personal narratives, stories, and biographies. (Note: biographies also inform.)

● **To Persuade**

To persuade means to convince someone else to agree with your opinion or goal, or to take action. Examples of writing to persuade include opinion paragraphs, persuasive essays, and book and film reviews.

Understanding Task, Audience, and Purpose (TAP)

Knowing your purpose is one way to help you select the type of writing you might do. You also have to consider your **audience**, or for whom you are writing. For example, the words you use in writing to a friend are likely to be different than those you use with someone you have never met.

Knowing your purpose and your audience will help you quickly select your **task**, or writing form. For example, if you want to tell your teacher and classmates about a topic you have been studying, you might choose to share the information as a report, an essay, or a multimedia presentation.

Decide your task, audience, and purpose, or **TAP**, before you begin writing. Your task is what you are writing. Your purpose is why you are writing. Your audience is for whom you are writing. Your teacher may give you the TAP for an assignment. Sometimes you will decide on your own.

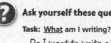 **Ask yourself these questions.**

Task: What am I writing?

Do I want to write a letter, a report, or something else?

Audience: For whom am I writing?

Am I writing for a teacher, a friend, myself, or someone else?

Purpose: Why am I writing?

Am I writing to persuade someone, to give information, or for another reasons?

● A closing paragraph that sums up and concludes.

Students will use this essay form to produce reports, literary analyses, theses, and critiques throughout their academic career. They will also be tested on their ability to write effective essays in standardized tests. In later life, as adults, they will need to be able to communicate clearly in writing to coworkers, bosses, and clients. This requires extensive and ongoing exposure to exemplary writing models and explicit instruction in a variety of areas, as well as opportunities to practice different forms of writing. In all cases, their purpose for writing must be clear. Evidence suggests that the more time student writers spend on writing, developing their writing skills, and deepening their writing experience, the better writers they become.

The Reading-Writing Connection

The ability to communicate their thinking about texts for a variety of purposes and audiences will serve students well in preparation for college and career readiness. When students write about what they read, reflecting on content, craft, or another aspect of a text, they provide evidence of their thinking. This helps teachers know how well students have understood a text. Additionally, the more students write in response to texts, the more they increase their ability to reflect and improve their critical writing ability. Also, students learn to cite evidence from texts in supporting their claims or supporting their main ideas. This ability becomes particularly useful in writing reports and opinion pieces.

Introduce the Purposes

Have students turn to page 8 and read the text. Explain that these are the key purposes for writing that will be explored in their handbooks. Give or elicit an example of a writing form that might be used for each purpose. Examples might include an informational paragraph or a research report *to inform*, directions or a how-to essay *to explain*, a story or personal narrative *to narrate*, and an opinion essay or letter to the editor *to persuade*. Then have students read the next page. Discuss how students should always consider their TAP—or task, audience, and purpose—to help them better target the message of their writing.

The Writing Process

The *Writing Handbook* presents the writing process as a strategy that students can use to help them write for any task, audience, or purpose. Students can use the writing process independently or as part of writing workshops in which they respond to each other's writing. The writing process can help students understand how to plan, write, and revise for various purposes and genres. It is thus useful in helping students meet academic standards for opinion, informative/explanatory, and narrative writing.

What Process Writing Is

The writing process, or process writing, is an instructional approach to writing that consists of five basic stages. The stages are prewriting, drafting, revising, editing, and publishing. The stages are recursive in nature, meaning that students are encouraged to go back and forth between the stages as needed.

The characteristics of the stages of the writing process are as follows:

Prewriting

This is the stage where students begin to plan their writing. Students:

- Define a task and purpose.
- Identify an audience.
- Brainstorm ideas.
- Narrow and choose a topic.
- Plan and organize information.

Drafting

During drafting, students make their first attempt at fleshing out the prewriting idea and forming it into a written work. In other words, students put their ideas in writing. In this stage, students:

- Write a first draft.
- Do not yet worry about perfecting their writing.

- Know that they can revise, edit, and proofread later.
- Use their plan and checklists to help them write or to return to prewriting, as needed.

Revising

A draft is reread and decisions are made to rework and improve it. In this stage, students might:

- Read aloud their work to others to determine how it sounds and how it might be improved.
- Conference with other students or their teachers.
- Add information.
- Delete unnecessary information.
- Rearrange sentences and paragraphs.
- Combine sentences.

Editing

During editing, the draft is polished. In this stage, students reread and correct their writing for the following:

- Grammar
- Spelling
- Mechanics
- Usage

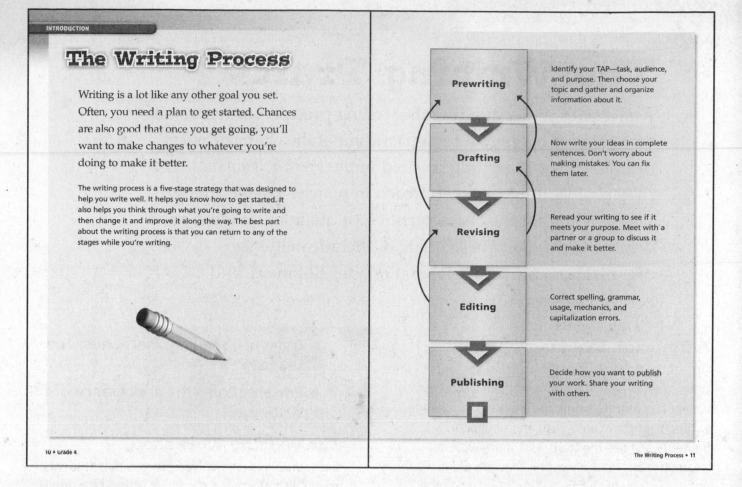

The Writing Process

Writing is a lot like any other goal you set. Often, you need a plan to get started. Chances are also good that once you get going, you'll want to make changes to whatever you're doing to make it better.

The writing process is a five-stage strategy that was designed to help you write well. It helps you know how to get started. It also helps you think through what you're going to write and then change it and improve it along the way. The best part about the writing process is that you can return to any of the stages while you're writing.

Prewriting
Identify your TAP—task, audience, and purpose. Then choose your topic and gather and organize information about it.

Drafting
Now write your ideas in complete sentences. Don't worry about making mistakes. You can fix them later.

Revising
Reread your writing to see if it meets your purpose. Meet with a partner or a group to discuss it and make it better.

Editing
Correct spelling, grammar, usage, mechanics, and capitalization errors.

Publishing
Decide how you want to publish your work. Share your writing with others.

Publishing

Students share their writing with others. In this stage, students typically:

- Make a final, clean copy.
- Use their best handwriting, if writing by hand. If they are sharing their work electronically, they typically choose typefaces and other elements to make their writing readable and attractive.
- Combine their writing with art or graphics.
- Make multiple copies, read their writing aloud, post it electronically, or share and display it in some other way.

Introduce the Process

Have students read pages 10–11. Explain that the writing process is a strategy that they can use to help them write about any topic. Point out how the graphic on page 11 has arrows, indicating that students can go back and forth between the stages as needed. For students who have no previous orientation to the writing process, simplify your introduction by emphasizing at first only the three key stages of planning, drafting, and revising. Elicit how most tasks of any nature require planning, doing or making something, and then thinking about what might be done better and making those improvements. Compare how these same basic stages can be used each time students write.

Have students turn to the table of contents and locate the section in their handbooks devoted to the writing process (pages 74–81). Explain that they can use these handbook pages whenever they need help with specific stages or writing in general. Point out that each stage in the handbook has one or two pages devoted to it that tell more about the stage. As an example, have students turn to the Prewriting pages 74–75, and point out how they show the different organizational plans students can use for the different kinds of writing they will do. Encourage students to use their handbooks as a resource whenever they write.

The Writing Traits

Along with understanding the writing process, students will benefit from having an understanding of the characteristics, or traits, of good writing covered in the *Writing Handbook*. The "Traits of Writing" is an approach in which students analyze their writing for the characteristics, or qualities, of what good writing looks like. These qualities include evidence, organization, purpose, elaboration, development, and conventions.

A Common Language

One of the advantages of instructing students in the traits of writing is that you give them a working vocabulary and thus build a common language for writing that they can all use and understand. Students can use the traits as a framework for improving any kind of writing they are doing. To this end, a systematic, explicitly taught focus on the traits of writing has proved to be an effective tool for discussing writing, enabling students to analyze and improve their own writing, and providing teachers with a way to assess students' compositions in a fair, even-handed manner.

Writers typically focus on six traits, with presentation—or the appearance of writing— sometimes considered an additional trait.

- **Evidence**—the details and examples that explain ideas and support opinions.
- **Organization**—the structure of the writing.
- **Purpose**—the reason for writing, which supports the type of writing and the audience.
- **Elaboration**—the words the writer uses to convey the message.
- **Development**—the advancement of a story through vivid details and interesting plot.
- **Conventions**—the correctness of the grammar, spelling, mechanics, and usage.
- **Presentation**—the appearance of the writing.

The Writing Workshop

Since writing is an involved process that students accomplish at varying speeds, it is usually a good idea to set aside a block of time for them to work on their writing. One time-tested model that has worked well in classrooms is the Writing Workshop. In this model during a set period of time, students work individually and collaboratively (with classmates and/or with the teacher) on different writing activities. One of these activities is for students to collaborate in reviewing each other's manuscripts. One effective technique used in many workshops as a way for students to comment on aspects of each other's writing is to use the language of the traits when they comment.

Some tasks are started and finished during a workshop, while others are ongoing. A writing workshop can serve many writing-related functions:

- Students can work on a class writing assignment (ongoing or quickly accomplished).
- Students can engage in independent writing, jotting down or consulting ideas in their writing log or journal, starting or working on pieces of their own devising.

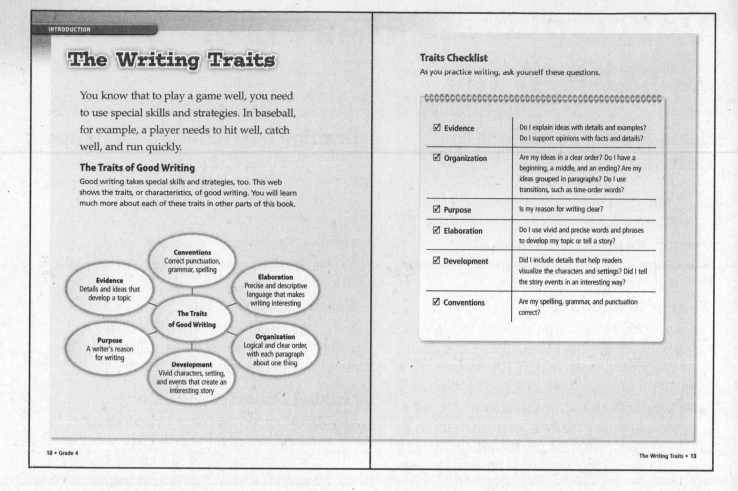

The Writing Traits

You know that to play a game well, you need to use special skills and strategies. In baseball, for example, a player needs to hit well, catch well, and run quickly.

The Traits of Good Writing

Good writing takes special skills and strategies, too. This web shows the traits, or characteristics, of good writing. You will learn much more about each of these traits in other parts of this book.

Conventions Correct punctuation, grammar, spelling

Evidence Details and ideas that develop a topic

Elaboration Precise and descriptive language that makes writing interesting

The Traits of Good Writing

Purpose A writer's reason for writing

Organization Logical and clear order, with each paragraph about one thing

Development Vivid characters, setting, and events that create an interesting story

12 • Grade 4

Traits Checklist

As you practice writing, ask yourself these questions.

☑ Evidence	Do I explain ideas with details and examples? Do I support opinions with facts and details?
☑ Organization	Are my ideas in a clear order? Do I have a beginning, a middle, and an ending? Are my ideas grouped in paragraphs? Do I use transitions, such as time-order words?
☑ Purpose	Is my reason for writing clear?
☑ Elaboration	Do I use vivid and precise words and phrases to develop my topic or tell a story?
☑ Development	Did I include details that help readers visualize the characters and settings? Did I tell the story events in an interesting way?
☑ Conventions	Are my spelling, grammar, and punctuation correct?

The Writing Traits • 13

- As previously mentioned, students can engage in peer-conferencing, giving one another advice about a piece of writing or sharing writing ideas.

- Students can select pieces for inclusion in their writing portfolio, where they keep their best work.

- Teachers can conference with individual students, reviewing student writing and discussing a given student's strengths and weaknesses as well as instructional progress.

- Teachers can engage in small-group instruction with students who need extra help with practice in specific areas of writing.

Writing Workshops are often most effective when they adhere to a dependable schedule and follow a set of clearly posted guidelines (for example, keep voices down, point out the good things about someone's writing as well as comment on aspects that might be revised, listen politely, put away materials when the workshop is over). In addition, students should know what areas of the classroom they can use during the Workshop and should have free access to writing materials, including their handbooks.

You may want to refer to the Writing Workshop pages in this *Writing Handbook Teacher's Guide* and teach one or two minilessons on writing workshop behaviors and activities so that students have a solid understanding of what is expected of them.

Introduce the Traits

Share the Writing Traits overview pages with students. Discuss each trait briefly and explain to students that their handbooks contain more information on the traits, which they can use to help them as they plan, draft, revise, edit, and publish their writing. Guide students to use their tables of content or indexes to locate where additional information can be found in their handbooks.

Descriptive Paragraph

Minilesson 1

Using Spatial Transitions to Describe

Objective: Use transitions in descriptive writing.

Guiding Question: How can transitions make my descriptions clear?

Teach/Model—I Do

Discuss handbook p. 14 with students; then point out the boldfaced transitions in the model. Explain that these are position words that tell where things are in relation to each other. Write sentences on the board, using transitions to describe the arrangement of the classroom. Underline the transitions. For example, _At the front_ of the room is the blackboard. _On the left_ is a window. _Below that_, my desk is pushed up against the wall.

Guided Practice—We Do

Arrange three or four objects at the front of the room, such as a chair, a desk, a book, and a pencil. Work with students to write sentences with transition words that describe the setup. For example, _In the front_, there is a desk. _On top of_ the desk is an open book. Help volunteers describe the placement of the other objects in logical order (such as left to right or top to bottom), using transition words. Write the sentences on the board.

Practice/Apply—You Do

COLLABORATIVE Have small groups look at a photograph or out a window. Have them use transition words in sentences to describe a few objects they see. Have them put sentences in a logical order.

INDEPENDENT Have students write two more sentences, continuing the description their group began.

Conference/Evaluate

If students have difficulty using position words, tell them to anchor their descriptions on one object. They can then use transitions to describe everything in relation to that object.

Minilesson 2

Drafting a Descriptive Paragraph

Objective: Write a descriptive paragraph.

Guiding Question: How can I help my audience see what I describe?

Teach/Model—I Do

Review the model with students, noting the topic and the details the writer included. Emphasize the use of vivid details and sensory words.

Guided Practice—We Do

 Direct students to Frame 1 on handbook p. 15. Have them suggest favorite places and then choose one familiar to all students. On the board, list details that students suggest, starting with the most noticeable feature of the place. Then guide students to suggest sentences, using the position words in the frame to describe features of the place. Have students write in their books as you write on the board.

Practice/Apply—You Do

COLLABORATIVE Have small groups plan and complete Frame 2. Have them decide on a familiar place and list its important features. They should then fill in the frame based on the spatial relationships among the features. Have groups share and discuss what they have written.

INDEPENDENT Have students read the directions. Tell them to use their prewriting plan from Lesson 1 or to brainstorm a new plan using Graphic Organizer 15.

Conference/Evaluate

As students draft, circulate and help them choose position words that make descriptions clear. Evaluate using the rubric on p. 104.

Digital
- eBook
- WriteSmart
- Interactive Lessons

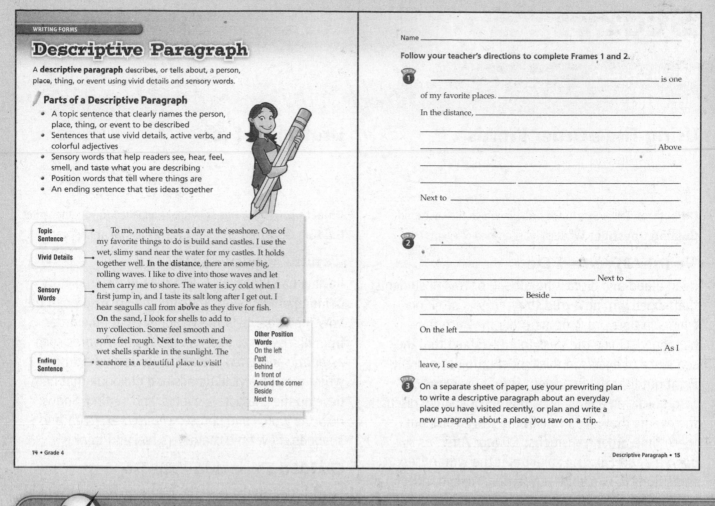

Descriptive Paragraph

A **descriptive paragraph** describes, or tells about, a person, place, thing, or event using vivid details and sensory words.

Parts of a Descriptive Paragraph

* A topic sentence that clearly names the person, place, thing, or event to be described
* Sentences that use vivid details, active verbs, and colorful adjectives
* Sensory words that help readers see, hear, feel, smell, and taste what you are describing
* Position words that tell where things are
* An ending sentence that ties ideas together

Topic Sentence	
Vivid Details	
Sensory Words	
Ending Sentence	

To me, nothing beats a day at the seashore. One of my favorite things to do is build sand castles. I use the wet, slimy sand near the water for my castles. It holds together well. **In the distance**, there are some big, rolling waves. I like to dive into those waves and let them carry me to shore. The water is icy cold when I first jump in, and I taste its salt long after I get out. I hear seagulls call from **above** as they dive for fish. **On the sand**, I look for shells to add to my collection. Some feel smooth and some feel rough. **Next** to the water, the wet shells sparkle in the sunlight. The seashore is a beautiful place to visit!

Other Position Words
On the left
Past
Behind
In front of
Around the corner
Beside
Next to

Name _____

Follow your teacher's directions to complete Frames 1 and 2.

1 _____ is one of my favorite places. _____

In the distance, _____

_____

_____ Above

Next to _____

_____

2 _____

_____

_____ Next to _____

_____ Beside _____

On the left _____

_____ As I

leave, I see _____

3 On a separate sheet of paper, use your prewriting plan to write a descriptive paragraph about an everyday place you have visited recently, or plan and write a new paragraph about a place you saw on a trip.

✔ Corrective Feedback

IF . . . students are unable to clearly describe the setting of their chosen place,

THEN . . . have them draw a picture of the place. This may help them visualize where objects are located in relation to one another. They can choose position words to describe where objects appear on their drawings.

Focus Trait: Elaboration

Remind students that using concrete, or exact, words makes writing more meaningful and helps create a picture in the reader's mind. On the board, write:

My friend and I went to see a show. When we got there, we smelled yummy food, so we got a bunch of stuff.

Point out that the sentence only gives a vague description of people, places, and things.

Work with students to rewrite the sentence using concrete words. Example:

My friend Leah and I biked to the movie theater. When we walked into the lobby, we smelled buttery popcorn, so we bought a bag of popcorn to share.

Minilesson 3	Minilesson 4

Using Time-Order Words

Objective: Tell events in the order in which they occurred.

Guiding Question: What is the sequence of events?

Teach/Model—I Do

Read aloud and discuss handbook p. 16. Tell students that, when writing a true story, writers often put events in time order, or the order in which they happened. Guide the class to understand that the sequence of events in this model unfolds naturally. Point out that the first event is that everyone but Jason picks an animal for a report topic. Then discuss the events that take place in the story. Point out these time-order transitions: *During, After, as soon as,* and *Finally.* Explain that the writer uses transitions to make the sequence of events clear to the reader.

Guided Practice—We Do

On the board, write these sentences: (1) *Jen looked on the floor under the seats.* (2) *Jen gave Pam her earring.* (3) *Pam lost one of her earrings on the bus.* Work with students to rewrite these events in the correct order (3, 1, 2). Then guide students to add transitional words or phrases that will make the time order more clear.

Practice/Apply—You Do

COLLABORATIVE Write these sentences on the board: *(1) The squirrel made a nest. (2) The squirrel collected leaves and twigs. (3) The squirrel slept in the nest.* Have groups rewrite these events in order (2, 1, 3), adding appropriate transitions.

INDEPENDENT Have students write three related events that happened to them, using time order and transitions.

Conference/Evaluate

Have students share their sequence of events with you to make sure they wrote them in the correct order.

Drafting a Story

Objective: Write a true story that happened to you, the writer.

Guiding Question: How do I tell readers what happened?

Teach/Model—I Do

Review handbook p. 16. Read aloud the true story, pointing out its beginning and ending. Also point out how the writer tells what happened in time order, from first event to last, using transition words such as *during* and *after.* Explain to students that the writer also uses vivid details and dialogue that help develop the characters, events, and setting. Show how the words and phrases *shouted excitedly* and *snapped* show how characters feel and think.

Guided Practice—We Do

 Direct students to the frame on handbook p. 17. Tell students that, together, you will write a true story about helping a friend solve a problem. Work with students to brainstorm real experiences. Ask *Whom did you help? What problem did this person face? How did you help this person?* Then, together, complete the frame, using time order and transitions. Have students write in their books as you write on the board.

Practice/Apply—You Do

 COLLABORATIVE Have groups plan and complete Activity 2. Remind them to use dialogue and descriptive details as well as time order and transitions. Have groups share their writing.

INDEPENDENT Have students read and follow the directions. Tell them to use their prewriting plan from Lesson 2 or to brainstorm a new plan using Graphic Organizer 4.

Conference/Evaluate

As students draft, have them evaluate their work using the rubric on p. 104.

Digital
- eBook
- WriteSmart
- Interactive Lessons

Story

A **story** tells about either a real or an imaginary experience or event. A true story tells about something that actually happened to the writer.

Parts of a Story

- A catchy beginning that introduces the main characters and the time and place of the story
- Events that are told in time order, or sequence
- Vivid details and dialogue that help readers understand the characters, events, and setting
- An ending that tells how the story worked out

Beginning
Makes readers want to find out more

On Thursday, everyone in our class picked animals for a report except Jason, who was out sick that day.

"It's not fair," Jason complained, "because *I* want to find out about leopards. Sara took my topic."

Events
Tell what happened in time order

During lunch, I tried to help Jason. I named a few interesting animals. None wowed him. **After lunch**, we went outside for gym. I spotted an odd creature **as soon as** I ran to the field. It crawled along the warm, red bricks of the school building.

Strong Details and Dialogue
Include sights, sounds, and the words characters say

"Hey, Jason, here's your science report!" I shouted excitedly, pointing to a thin, brown twig.

"We're studying animals," Jason snapped.

"That walking stick *is* an insect," I explained.

Ending
Wraps up the story and tells how the writer felt

Jason grinned. **Finally**, he had a subject he liked! I felt proud to help my friend.

Other Transitions
First
Next
Then
During
Meanwhile
Later
Last
Until

Name _____

Follow your teacher's directions to complete the frame.

1 A problem that I helped a friend solve was _____

_____

First, _____

_____ Then _____

_____

_____ Next, _____

_____

_____

_____

_____ Later, _____

_____ After that, _____

_____

_____ Finally, _____

I felt _____

2 On a separate sheet of paper, write a true story about the funniest joke you ever played on someone.

3 On a separate sheet of paper, use your prewriting plan to write a true story, or make a new plan to write about a time when you stood up for something you believe in.

Corrective Feedback

IF . . . students are having a hard time coming up with vivid details,

THEN . . . have them visualize what they are trying to describe and use their five senses to capture how people, places, or things look, feel, taste, sound, or smell. For example, the words *frowned*, *slammed the locker*, and *stomped noisily* use words related to the senses of sight and sound to help show that a character felt angry.

Focus Trait: Elaboration

Tell students that an interesting true story includes words that describe and elaborate on the plot. Explain that good writers choose strong words to describe the different parts of a story: the characters, events, and setting. These words will help readers understand what happened.

Refer students to a true story they have read in a magazine or newspaper, in their textbooks, or in another book. Ask them to identify examples of strong words that help readers understand the characters, events, or setting.

Then write these sentences the board:

Tim ate a sandwich. He felt satisfied.

Have students rewrite the two sentences using stronger, more descriptive words. For example:

Tim ate a gooey, grilled-cheese sandwich.

He didn't leave a single crumb on his plate.

Dialogue

Minilesson 5

Using Dialogue to Show Characters' Feelings

Objective: Use dialogue to show characters' feelings.

Guiding Question: How can I show how characters feel?

Teach/Model—I Do

Read aloud and discuss handbook p. 18, noting that dialogue is the exact words characters say in a story. Explain that dialogue often shows how characters feel and that, in this model, dialogue shows Grandma's response to a jellyfish. The writer uses the words *Don't move* and *hissed* to show that Grandma feels frightened. Discuss other words in the model that show how the characters feel.

Guided Practice—We Do

Tell students to imagine that one friend is giving another a birthday present. Work with students to create a dialogue between the two characters that shows how pleased one friend is to receive the gift and how happy the other friend is that it is appreciated. Write suggestions on the board and help students sharpen the dialogue to better reflect the two characters' feelings.

Practice/Apply—You Do

COLLABORATIVE Have small groups work together to write dialogue for the following situation. One friend invites another to come play, but the other friend has to do chores for her mother. Groups should share their work with other groups, making constructive suggestions for improvements.

INDEPENDENT Have students write two or three lines of dialogue between two characters that show one of the characters feels worried.

Conference/Evaluate

Have students think about whether their dialogue conveys a character's feelings.

Minilesson 6

Drafting Dialogue

Objective: Write dialogue.

Guiding Question: How do I write dialogue?

Teach/Model—I Do

Review handbook p. 18. Read aloud the model and identify examples of dialogue. Explain that speaker's tags (boldfaced in the model) tell *who* is speaking. Writers bring dialogue to life by adding actions, movements, and descriptions that tell *how* a character speaks. Good dialogue uses words people would actually say in real life. Point out the punctuation the writer used to set off dialogue.

Guided Practice—We Do

We Do 1 Direct students to the frame on handbook p. 19. Tell students that, together, you will write dialogue. With students, brainstorm a conversation between two characters and then complete the frame. Help students use words that sound natural and show what a character is like. Have students write in their books as you write on the board.

Practice/Apply—You Do

You Do 2 **COLLABORATIVE** Have groups plan and complete Activity 2. Remind them to use proper punctuation. Have groups share what they have written.

You Do 3 **INDEPENDENT** Have students read the directions. Tell them to use their prewriting plan from Lesson 3 or to make a new plan. Have them use Graphic Organizer 1 with column headings *Thoughts, Actions, Words.*

Conference/Evaluate

As students draft, have them evaluate their work using the rubric on p. 104.

Digital
• eBook
• WriteSmart
• Interactive Lessons

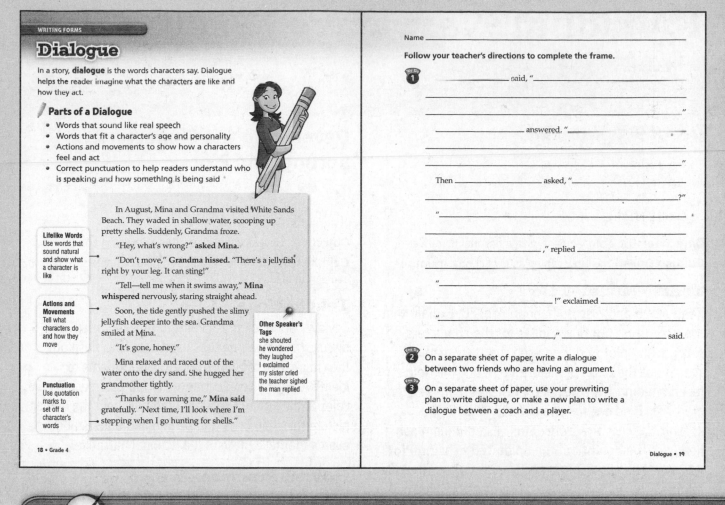

Dialogue

In a story, **dialogue** is the words characters say. Dialogue helps the reader imagine what the characters are like and how they act.

Parts of a Dialogue

- Words that sound like real speech
- Words that fit a character's age and personality
- Actions and movements to show how a characters feel and act
- Correct punctuation to help readers understand who is speaking and how something is being said

Lifelike Words
Use words that sound natural and show what a character is like

Actions and Movements
Tell what characters do and how they move

Punctuation
Use quotation marks to set off a character's words

In August, Mina and Grandma visited White Sands Beach. They waded in shallow water, scooping up pretty shells. Suddenly, Grandma froze.

"Hey, what's wrong?" **asked Mina.**

"Don't move," **Grandma hissed.** "There's a jellyfish right by your leg. It can sting!"

"Tell—tell me when it swims away," **Mina whispered** nervously, staring straight ahead.

Soon, the tide gently pushed the slimy jellyfish deeper into the sea. Grandma smiled at Mina.

"It's gone, honey."

Mina relaxed and raced out of the water onto the dry sand. She hugged her grandmother tightly.

"Thanks for warning me," **Mina said** gratefully. "Next time, I'll look where I'm stepping when I go hunting for shells."

Other Speaker's Tags
she shouted
he wondered
they laughed
I exclaimed
my sister cried
the teacher sighed
the man replied

Name _____

Follow your teacher's directions to complete the frame.

1 _____ said, "_____
_____
_____ "

_____ answered, "_____
_____
_____ "

Then _____ asked, "_____
_____?"

"_____

_____," replied _____

"_____

_____ !" exclaimed _____

"_____

_____," _____ said.

2 On a separate sheet of paper, write a dialogue between two friends who are having an argument.

3 On a separate sheet of paper, use your prewriting plan to write dialogue, or make a new plan to write a dialogue between a coach and a player.

✓ Corrective Feedback

IF . . . students are having a hard time making their dialogue sound natural,

THEN . . . have pairs role play the characters and say the dialogue aloud. Direct students to make changes to help the dialogue reflect the characters' ages and personalities as well as to make the words sound more true to life.

✎ Focus Trait: Elaboration

Tell students that elaboration is the writer's choice of words he or she uses to convey a message. The writer's words can show characters' feelings and personalities.

Explain that natural-sounding dialogue is often informal and lifelike. For example, it might include slang or sentence fragments.

Refer students to examples of dialogue in their textbook or in another book. Have them analyze the way the writer shows how characters feel.

Then write the following sentences on the board. Have students turn them into dialogue, using an appropriate voice for each character:

Carl asked his teacher for a pencil. Mr. Rich handed him a sharp pencil and told him to be careful.

For example:

"Could I borrow a pencil?" Carl asked politely.

"Watch out! It's got a sharp point," warned Mr. Rich.

Fictional Narrative: Prewriting

Minilesson 7	**Minilesson 8**

Using a Story Map

Objective: Use a story map to plan a fictional narrative.

Guiding Question: How can I plan my fictional narrative?

Teach/Model—I Do

Read aloud and discuss handbook p. 20. Explain that the writer first put down ideas for the characters, setting, and plot and then used the story map to sketch out the parts of a story. Point out the bold-faced headings **Setting** and **Characters** in the story map. Ask *Who are the characters? What is the setting?* Discuss the story details listed under each heading. Then point out the boldfaced heading **Plot**. Ask *What happens in the beginning of the story? the middle? the ending? What is the climax?* Guide students to understand that a story map is a kind of outline that they can use to plan and organize fictional narratives.

Guided Practice—We Do

On the board, write these story elements: (1) *John loses his backpack at school.* (2) *Pine Valley School* (3) *Mr. Rizzi helps John look for his backpack.* (4) *Mr. Rizzi and John* (5) *John thanks Mr. Rizzi.* (6) *Mr. Rizzi finds John's backpack behind the closed stage curtains.* Work with students to put the Setting, Characters, Beginning, Middle, Climax, and Ending into a story map.

Practice/Apply—You Do

COLLABORATIVE Have groups choose a story they have recently read. Then have them put the parts of the story into a story map.

INDEPENDENT Have students choose another story and put the elements into a story map.

Conference/Evaluate

Have students examine their lists to make sure they can use each of these elements in a story map.

Developing the Characters, Setting, and Plot

Objective: Develop story characters, setting, and plot.

Guiding Question: How can I bring the characters, setting, and plot to life?

Teach/Model—I Do

Review handbook p. 20. Point to the story map and discuss how the writer has used details to flesh out the characters, setting, and plot. Ask students to identify specific details that the writer lists, such as the color of the kitten. Explain that details help the reader picture the characters and setting and understand events that take place in the fictional narrative.

Guided Practice—We Do

We Do 1 Direct students to handbook p. 21. Tell students that, together, you will complete a story map about someone who begs her mother for permission to do something, such as babysit. Work with students to brainstorm characters, setting, and plot events. Then, together, complete the map with students' suggestions. Help students fill in each section of the story map with vivid details. Have students write in their books as you write on the board.

Practice/Apply—You Do

You Do 2 **COLLABORATIVE** Have groups plan and complete Activity 2. Have them create a story map and then share what they have written.

You Do 3 **INDEPENDENT** Have students read and follow the directions. Tell them to use their prewriting plan from Lesson 4 or another plan they create using Graphic Organizer 10.

Conference/Evaluate

As students draft, have them evaluate their work using the rubric on p. 104.

 Digital
- eBook
- WriteSmart
- Interactive Lessons

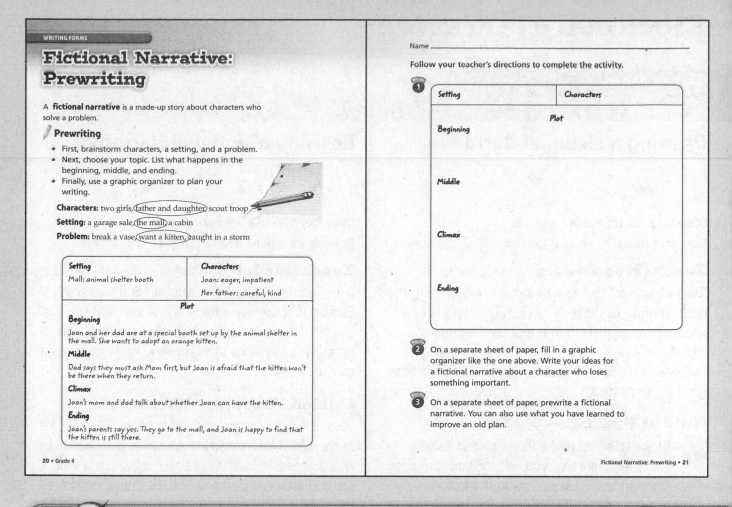

Fictional Narrative: Prewriting

A **fictional narrative** is a made-up story about characters who solve a problem.

✏ Prewriting

- First, brainstorm characters, a setting, and a problem.
- Next, choose your topic. List what happens in the beginning, middle, and ending.
- Finally, use a graphic organizer to plan your writing.

Characters: two girls, ~~father and daughter~~ scout troop

Setting: a garage sale, ~~the mall~~ a cabin

Problem: break a vase, ~~want a kitten~~ caught in a storm

Setting	Characters
Mall: animal shelter booth	Joan: eager, impatient
	Her father: careful, kind

Plot

Beginning
Joan and her dad are at a special booth set up by the animal shelter in the mall. She wants to adopt an orange kitten.

Middle
Dad says they must ask Mom first, but Joan is afraid that the kitten won't be there when they return.

Climax
Joan's mom and dad talk about whether Joan can have the kitten.

Ending
Joan's parents say yes. They go to the mall, and Joan is happy to find that the kitten is still there.

Name _____

Follow your teacher's directions to complete the activity.

1

Setting	Characters

Plot

Beginning

Middle

Climax

Ending

2 On a separate sheet of paper, fill in a graphic organizer like the one above. Write your ideas for a fictional narrative about a character who loses something important.

3 On a separate sheet of paper, prewrite a fictional narrative. You can also use what you have learned to improve an old plan.

✓ Corrective Feedback

IF . . . students find it difficult to develop details for the characters, setting, or plot,

THEN . . . have them visualize what they are trying to describe. Tell them that details from these mental pictures can be used in their story maps and that they can help bring these story elements to life. For example, the setting might be *a musty historical museum crammed with antique furniture, rusty tools, and old-fashioned clothing.*

✎ Focus Trait: Development

To help students think of ways to develop their fictional narratives, guide them to think of and list settings that interest them. For example:

A spooky, haunted old castle

The beach on a rainy day

A soccer field

Have students choose the setting that most interests them. Have them imagine what characters would be in this setting and what problems the characters would encounter there. Have students write their ideas into a story map.

Fictional Narrative

Minilesson 9

Drafting a Fictional Narrative

Objective: Draft a fictional narrative.

Guiding Question: How can I write a fictional narrative?

Teach/Model—I Do

Read aloud and discuss handbook p. 22. Refer to the callouts and ask students to identify the parts of a fictional narrative. Point out that the beginning introduces a problem and often includes dialogue that draws readers in, making them want to find out what happens next.

Guided Practice—We Do

 Direct students to the frame on handbook p. 23. Tell them that you will use your prewriting plan from Lesson 4 to draft a fictional narrative. Together, review your plans for a story about a persistent child who begs her mother for permission to do something, such as babysit. Guide students to add more details about events that might take place. Then complete the frame together. Have students write in their books as you write on the board.

Practice/Apply—You Do

 COLLABORATIVE Have groups complete Activity 2 using their prewriting plans from Minilesson 8. Remind them to build up to an exciting point that will be the climax.

INDEPENDENT Have students read and follow the directions for Activity 3. Tell them to use their prewriting plan from Minilesson 8 or to brainstorm a new plan using Graphic Organizer 10.

Conference/Evaluate

As students draft, have them evaluate their work using the rubric on p. 104.

Minilesson 10

Revising a Fictional Narrative

Objective: Revise a fictional narrative.

Guiding Question: How can I improve my narrative?

Teach/Model—I Do

Point out the boldfaced words on handbook p. 22. Explain that these are transition words that signal a change in time. Note that transition words like these establish a sequence of events and keep the fictional narrative moving along in a logical way.

Guided Practice—We Do

Write these sentences on the board: *Jeff decided to make a kite. He created a frame with wooden sticks. He covered the frame with paper. He made a long tail and attached it to one end. To the other end, he attached a flying line so that he could fly the kite. He went to a windy field.* Work with students to add transitions that will help readers follow the sequence of events *(first, then, next)*.

Practice/Apply—You Do

COLLABORATIVE Ask students to work in groups to circle the transitions in their drafts from Minilesson 9. Then have them suggest places to add other transitions.

INDEPENDENT Have students use suggestions from their groups to revise their drafts from Minilesson 9. Encourage them to add variety by using transitional phrases as well.

Conference/Evaluate

As students revise, help them determine whether their narratives move smoothly from one part to the next. Evaluate their work using the rubric on p. 104.

Digital
- eBook
- WriteSmart
- Interactive Lessons

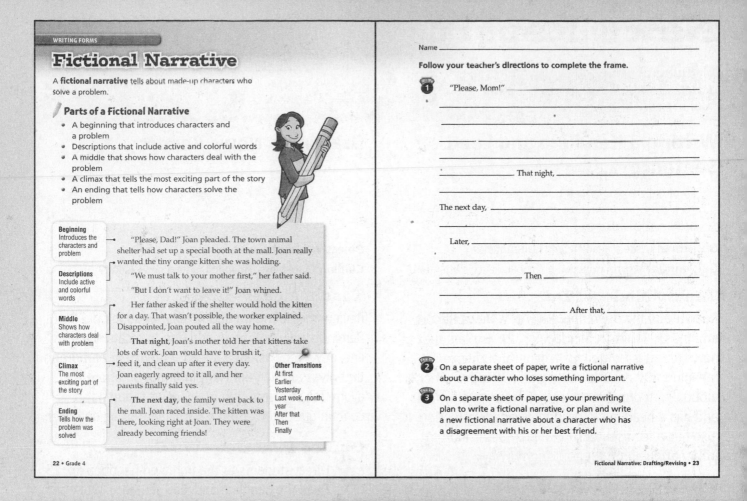

Fictional Narrative

A **fictional narrative** tells about made-up characters who solve a problem.

Parts of a Fictional Narrative

- A beginning that introduces characters and a problem
- Descriptions that include active and colorful words
- A middle that shows how characters deal with the problem
- A climax that tells the most exciting part of the story
- An ending that tells how characters solve the problem

Beginning
Introduces the characters and problem

Descriptions
Include active and colorful words

Middle
Shows how characters deal with problem

Climax
The most exciting part of the story

Ending
Tells how the problem was solved

"Please, Dad!" Joan pleaded. The town animal shelter had set up a special booth at the mall. Joan really wanted the tiny orange kitten she was holding.

"We must talk to your mother first," her father said.

"But I don't want to leave it!" Joan whined.

Her father asked if the shelter would hold the kitten for a day. That wasn't possible, the worker explained. Disappointed, Joan pouted all the way home.

That night, Joan's mother told her that kittens take lots of work. Joan would have to brush it, feed it, and clean up after it every day. Joan eagerly agreed to it all, and her parents finally said yes.

The next day, the family went back to the mall. Joan raced inside. The kitten was there, looking right at Joan. They were already becoming friends!

Other Transitions
At first
Earlier
Yesterday
Last week, month, year
After that
Then
Finally

Name _____

Follow your teacher's directions to complete the frame.

1 "Please, Mom!" _____

_____

_____

_____ That night, _____

The next day, _____

Later, _____

_____ Then _____

_____ After that, _____

2 On a separate sheet of paper, write a fictional narrative about a character who loses something important.

3 On a separate sheet of paper, use your prewriting plan to write a fictional narrative, or plan and write a new fictional narrative about a character who has a disagreement with his or her best friend.

✓ Corrective Feedback

IF . . . students have difficulty using transitions to establish the sequence of events,

THEN . . . have them review their completed story maps to identify places where the time or setting changes. Tell them to add appropriate words and phrases at these points of transition.

Focus Trait: Organization

Remind students that fictional narratives are organized with a clear beginning, middle, and ending. Explain that the setting, characters, and problem are introduced in the beginning.

On the board, write this beginning to a fictional narrative:

"Oww, my leg," Claire moaned. After skidding on a patch of gravel, she had fallen and couldn't get up. Unfortunately, the bike path was deserted, and her sister Julia was far ahead.

Have students identify the setting *(a deserted bike path)*, characters *(Claire and Julia)*, and problem *(Claire had a bike accident and can't get up)*.

Explain that the middle of a good fictional narrative often includes hints or clues about what the ending will be. Point out that these clues help readers make sense of the events so that the ending is logical.

Remind students that the ending should tell how the problem was resolved.

News Report

Minilesson 11

Writing a Headline and Lead Sentence

Objective: Write a headline and lead sentence.

Guiding Question: How do I get my audience's attention?

Teach/Model—I Do

Read aloud the definition, Parts of a News Report, and 5Ws + H list on handbook p. 24. Explain that a news report is written for a general audience, meaning that anyone could read it. Read the model aloud. Point out that the report presents only facts and has a headline to grab the reader's attention. It also has a lead sentence that provides important information about the topic right away.

Guided Practice—We Do

Work with students to come up with a list of recent special school events, such as a concert or fundraiser. List the events on the board. Guide students to choose one event and write a headline about it to grab the reader's attention, such as *Fourth-Graders Make Beautiful Music*. Then, together, write a lead sentence with a few important facts about the event, such as *The students in Mrs. Lopez's fourth-grade class played in a concert on May 14.*

Practice/Apply—You Do

COLLABORATIVE Have small groups work together to choose another event from the list and write a headline. Then have them write a lead sentence with a few important facts to go with the headline.

INDEPENDENT Have students work on their own to choose another event from the board and write a headline. Then have them write a lead sentence with a few important facts to go with that headline.

Conference/Evaluate

Circulate and offer help as needed. If students struggle to write a headline, have them think about what the most exciting part of the event was. They can describe that part in the headline.

Minilesson 12

Drafting a News Report

Objective: Write a news report.

Guiding Question: How do I write a news report?

Teach/Model—I Do

Review the definition and list on handbook p. 24. Remind students that, in addition to a catchy headline, news reports need a lead sentence or paragraph that gives all the important information about the event. Tell students that many news reports also contain quotations from a participant or an onlooker.

Guided Practice—We Do

We Do 1 Direct students to the frame on handbook p. 25. Read the headline and lead sentence. Work with students to come up with possible facts for the news report, such as *Students started a recycling program*. Then guide students to suggest a quotation to support the facts, such as *One student said, "It is really exciting to win this award."* Use students' suggestions to complete the report. Have students write in their books as you write on the board.

Practice/Apply—You Do

You Do 2 **COLLABORATIVE** Have small groups work together to complete Activity 2. Remind them to write a catchy headline and to include all the important information. Have groups share their work.

You Do 3 **INDEPENDENT** Have students read and follow the directions for Activity 3.

Conference/Evaluate

As students draft, remind them to include only facts in their news reports. Have students evaluate using the rubric on p. 104.

 Digital
- eBook
- WriteSmart
- Interactive Lessons

News Report

A **news report** tells about a real event that happened recently.

Parts of a News Report

- A headline, or title, that uses strong words to catch the reader's attention
- A lead, or beginning paragraph, that introduces the most important information in an interesting way
- A body that gives true information about the event and answers the questions *who, what, when, where, why,* and *how*
- A quotation from a participant or an onlooker, if possible

Headline Catches reader's attention	**St. Petersburg Student Wins Science Award**
	By Marsha Sanders, March 12, 2013
Interesting Lead	Tampa—Wesley Jackson, a fourth-grader from St. Petersburg, won the Curie Science Award. His entry was a simple robot that picks up and moves books and other objects.
Body Gives information about the event	The award is given every year to one student who participates in the Statewide School Science Fair. Jackson was one of 54 students to enter the contest.
	"We were excited by his work," said Thomas Garrett, a teacher who judged at the fair.
Quotation Actual words of people who saw the event	"I am happy all my hard work paid off," said Jackson. He plans to use the prize money to build another robot.

5 Ws + H
Who
What
When
Where
Why
How

Name _____

Follow your teacher's directions to complete the frame.

1 Local School Goes Green, Wins Big
The governor of Florida gave a prize to Jefferson Elementary School in Gainsville for being friendly to the environment.

_____
_____
_____
_____

One student said, "_____
_____."
_____
_____
_____
_____
_____
_____

2 On a separate sheet of paper, plan and write a news report about a school play or sporting event you attended.

3 On a separate sheet of paper, plan and write a news report about an event that took place in your town.

Corrective Feedback

IF . . . students have trouble writing a lead,

THEN . . . have them think about the questions *Who? What? When? Where? Why? How?* Remind students that their news reports should answer all of these questions. For example, for a basketball report, *Who* is the basketball team. *What* is the game they won. *Where* is the town the game took place. *Why* might be that the team had a talented player. *How* might be that the team worked hard and held extra practices.

Focus Trait: Evidence

An interview is an important writing type in which to get evidence for a news report. Tell students that whenever possible, they should interview people who observed or participated in the event that the report discusses. Advise students to write a list of questions in advance and to bring paper and a pen or pencil to record what the person says. Write the following questions on the board:

When and where did the event take place? Who else was there? What did you see, hear, and smell? How did you feel?

Have students practice interviewing each other about a recent school event, using the questions above as a guide. Encourage students to ask follow-up questions.

Informational Paragraph

Minilesson 13

Developing a Topic with Details and Examples

Objective: Use details and examples to develop a topic.

Guiding Question: What details will I use to inform my readers?

Teach/Model—I Do

Read aloud and discuss handbook p. 26. Explain that details and examples help the writer explain the topic. On the board, write this sentence from the model: *Later, ancient Greeks rolled metal hoops with a short stick.* Point out that these details help readers understand how children in Greece played with hoops long ago and what the hoops looked like. Discuss other details and examples that the writer uses in this informational paragraph to help readers understand this topic.

Guided Practice—We Do

On the board, write a sports topic that your students are familiar with, such as *baseball*. Work with students to list details and examples that develop the topic. Guide them to think about how many players are on a team, how and where the sport is played, what equipment is needed, and so on.

Practice/Apply—You Do

COLLABORATIVE Write other sports topics on the board, such as *soccer*, *basketball*, *football*, or *skateboarding*. Have groups choose one topic and then list details and examples they would use to develop it.

INDEPENDENT Have students choose another informational topic and then list related details and examples on their own.

Conference/Evaluate

Have students share their lists with you to make sure they chose relevant details and examples to develop their topics.

Minilesson 14

Drafting an Informational Paragraph

Objective: Write a paragraph to inform readers.

Guiding Question: How will I explain my subject?

Teach/Model—I Do

Review handbook p. 26. Read aloud the model and point out the main idea in the first sentence: *Playing with hoops is a very old custom.* Remind students that the writer uses supporting details to develop the main idea. Finally, point out the conclusion of the paragraph, which restates the main idea.

Guided Practice—We Do

We Do 1 Direct students to the frame on handbook p. 27. Tell students that together you will write an informational paragraph about your school. Work with students to draft a topic sentence, such as *Our school is trying to be "greener."* Then, together, complete the frame with facts, examples, and other details. Help students write a conclusion that sums up the main idea. Have students write in their books as you write on the board.

Practice/Apply—You Do

You Do 2 **COLLABORATIVE** Have groups plan and complete Activity 2. Tell them they can write about where this food comes from, what it looks like, and so on. Have groups share what they have written.

You Do 3 **INDEPENDENT** Have students read and follow the directions. Tell them to use their prewriting plan from Lesson 7 or brainstorm a new plan using Graphic Organizer 15.

Conference/Evaluate

As students draft, have them evaluate their work using the rubric on p. 104.

 Digital
• eBook
• WriteSmart
• Interactive Lessons

Informational Paragraph

An **informational paragraph** explains a subject, gives directions, or tells a reader how to do something. It includes facts, examples, definitions, and other details.

Parts of an Informational Paragraph

- A topic sentence that introduces the main idea
- Supporting details that develop the main idea
- Use of precise words
- An ending that sums up the main idea

Topic sentence Introduces the main idea

Supporting Details Give facts, examples, and other information

Precise Words Use words and phrases that clearly convey ideas

Ending Sums up the main idea

Playing with hoops is a very old custom. Long ago, children in Europe, the Americas, Africa, and Asia played with hoops. **For example**, by about 1,000 B.C., children in Egypt rolled large hoops made of dried vines. Later, ancient Greeks rolled metal hoops with a short stick. They decorated their hoops with bells. Ancient Romans and Native Americans used a hoop as a target. They threw spears through it as it rolled. In other cultures, children had hoop races. Teams sometimes played hoop battles. Players who knocked down the most hoops would win. **Also**, children played entertaining games of skill. They made gates by setting two bricks or stones a few inches apart. Then they tried to get their hoops through the narrow gates without touching the sides. Games like these have made playing with hoops popular around the world for thousands of years.

Other Transitions
In addition
Furthermore
As well
Such as
Besides
Likewise
Another
Moreover
However

Name _____

Follow your teacher's directions to complete the frame.

1 _____
_____

For instance, _____
_____
_____
_____
_____
_____

_____ such as _____
_____

_____ In addition, _____
_____
_____

_____ Also, _____
_____

2 On a separate sheet of paper, write an informational paragraph about your favorite kind of food.

3 On a separate sheet of paper, use your prewriting plan to write an informational paragraph, or make a new plan to write about a famous monument.

Corrective Feedback

IF . . . students are having a hard time finding supporting details,

THEN . . . have them refer to an encyclopedia or other reference books or interview someone who knows about the topic. Encourage them to look for statistics, quotations, and other interesting facts.

Focus Trait: Elaboration

Tell students that an informational paragraph includes words that help to elaborate on details the writer wants to convey. Explain that good writers elaborate on their ideas by choosing exact words to describe people, places, things, or events. Point out that precise words in the model, such as *vines* and *two bricks or stones*, clearly convey what the writer wants to say.

Now refer students to an informational paragraph in their science or social studies textbook. Ask them to

volunteer examples of precise words that help them better understand the topic.

Then write these sentences on the board:

Some frogs make loud sounds with their body parts.

Spring peepers *make loud* peeping *sounds with their* vocal sacs.

Guide students to understand that precise words in the second sentence help readers understand the topic.

Book Report

Minilesson 15

Summarizing Information

Objective: Summarize information.

Guiding Question: Which details should I include in a summary?

Teach/Model—I Do

Read aloud and discuss handbook p. 28. Explain that an important part of a book report is the *summary*, a short retelling that lets readers know what a book is about. To summarize this story, for example, the writer tells about the characters *(Lily, Charlie, judge)*, setting *(Brooklyn, New York; a tiny studio)*, and important events. Make a chart that lists the important parts of the book.

Guided Practice—We Do

On the board, write a three-column chart with these headings: *Characters, Setting, Events.* Work with students to complete the chart. First, choose a story that the class has recently read together. Then guide students to list the main characters, setting, and most important events in the story.

Practice/Apply—You Do

COLLABORATIVE Write several other story titles on the board. Have groups choose a story they remember well and then make a chart that includes the main characters, the setting, and the most important events.

INDEPENDENT Have students choose another story from the board and make a chart that lists the important parts of it.

Conference/Evaluate

Have students review their summary charts to make sure they included the most important story elements.

Minilesson 16

Drafting a Book Report

Objective: Write a book report.

Guiding Question: How do I tell readers about a book I have read?

Teach/Model—I Do

Review handbook p. 28. Read the model aloud and point out the information the writer gives about *Charlie's Paintbrush*, including the title, the author, and the kind of book. Point out the summary in the second and third paragraphs, explaining that the writer gives just a few key details that help readers understand who and what the book is about.

Guided Practice—We Do

We Do 1 Direct students to the frame on handbook p. 29. Tell students that, together, you will write a book report. Have students choose a book they have read. Then, together, complete the frame, beginning with this sentence: _____ *is a* _____ *story by* _____. Help students summarize important story elements. Have students write in their books as you write on the board.

Practice/Apply—You Do

You Do 2 COLLABORATIVE For Activity 2, have groups use their charts from Minilesson 15 to draft a book report. Have groups share what they have written.

You Do 3 INDEPENDENT Have students read and follow the directions. Tell them to use their prewriting plan from Lesson 8 or to brainstorm a new plan using Graphic Organizer 10.

Conference/Evaluate

As students draft, have them evaluate their work using the rubric on p. 104.

 Digital
- eBook
- WriteSmart
- Interactive Lessons

Book Report

A book report is a summary of what a book is about, where it takes place, and what happens. It helps readers understand what a particular book is about.

Parts of a Book Report

- An introduction that clearly states the main idea
- A body that tells about the most important parts of the book
- A conclusion that sums up the book

Introduction
States the title, the author, and the kind of book

→ *Charlie's Paintbrush* is a fictional story by Beth Cody. The book is about a talented artist named Lily. Lily's dream is to go to art school.

Body
Tells about main characters, setting, and events

→ Every day, Lily takes the train to Brooklyn, New York. She paints in a tiny studio. One afternoon, a stray cat with a puffy tail visits her. Lily names the cat Charlie. **After** Charlie's fourth visit, Lily finds a long purple streak across the middle of her new painting. **Next**, she finds red paint smeared along the bottom. Who ruined her painting? She has no idea, so she sets a trap to find out. **Finally**, Lily realizes that Charlie thinks he is an artist, too.

Conclusion
Restates the title and author of the book

→ **Later**, Lily enters her new painting in an art contest. The judge likes the bold way she uses a paintbrush. Lily—and Charlie—win first prize. Read *Charlie's Paintbrush* by Beth Cody yourself to find out what Lily does with the prize money!

Other Transitions
First
Now
After that
During
After a while
Meanwhile
Then
Last

Name _____

Follow your teacher's directions to complete the frame.

1 _____

_____ At first,

_____

_____ Then _____

_____

_____

_____ Next, _____

_____

_____

_____

_____

_____ After that, _____

_____

_____

_____ Finally, _____

_____

_____

2 On a separate sheet of paper, write a book report about a fictional book you have recently read.

3 On a separate sheet of paper, use your prewriting plan to write a book report, or make a new plan to write one about a book that tells about a real person in history.

✔ Corrective Feedback

IF . . . students are having a hard time summarizing the book,

THEN . . . have them create a three-column chart to list *all* of the characters, settings, and events in the book. Have them draw a line through any story elements that are *not* essential to a reader's understanding of the book.

Focus Trait: Organization

Tell students that a book report has a particular organization. It consists of three or more paragraphs, and each paragraph has a different purpose.

- A book report begins with an *introduction* that states the main idea.

- The *body* is one or more paragraphs that summarize the most important elements of the book.

- The *conclusion* sums up the book and restates the title and author.

Refer students to the model. Have them identify the three different parts of the book report about *Charlie's Paintbrush*, reading each part aloud.

Explanatory Essay: Prewriting

Deciding *What*, *Why*, and *How*

Objective: Decide which facts and details to use.
Guiding Question: What information do I need to include?

Teach/Model—I Do
Read aloud and discuss handbook p. 30. Have students look at the idea-support map. Point out the topic: *Children's Day in Japan*. Note that the writer includes details that answer these questions about the topic: *What* is Children's Day? *Why* is Children's Day celebrated? *How* is Children's Day celebrated? Discuss the facts and examples in the idea-support map that answer *what*, *why*, and *how*.

Guided Practice—We Do
On the board, write the topic *International Space Station*. Help students formulate questions about this topic. For example, they might ask *What* is the International Space Station? *Why* was it created? *How* does it gather information about space? Explain that asking *what*, *why*, and *how* helps writers decide which kinds of information belong in their explanatory essays.

Practice/Apply—You Do
COLLABORATIVE Have groups choose a topic for an explanatory essay and list facts and details about the topic that tell *what*, *why*, and *how*. Have them circle the information they would use in an essay.

INDEPENDENT Have students choose another explanatory topic and make a list of three facts or details they would include in an essay.

Conference/Evaluate
Have students share their lists with you to check that they have made appropriate decisions.

Organizing an Explanatory Essay

Objective: Determine a logical organization.
Guiding Question: How do I organize my essay?

Teach/Model—I Do
Review handbook p. 30. Have students look at the three main ideas in the idea-support map. Guide them to understand how the writer supports each main idea with facts and examples. Point out that each paragraph in an explanatory essay focuses on one main idea; all of the sentences in the paragraph tell about that idea.

Guided Practice—We Do
We Do 1 Direct students to Activity 1 on handbook p. 31. Tell them that, together, you will create an idea-support map. Work with students to brainstorm a familiar holiday from another culture and write this topic at the top of the map. For example, you might write *The Day of the Dead in Mexico*. Then, together, complete the frame with main ideas and supporting facts and details. Have students write in their books as you write on the board.

Practice/Apply—You Do
You Do 2 **COLLABORATIVE** Have groups plan and complete Activity 2 in which they create an idea-support map about their topic and then share what they have written.

You Do 3 **INDEPENDENT** Have students read and follow the directions. Tell them to use their prewriting plan from Lesson 9 or to brainstorm a new plan using Graphic Organizer 7.

Conference/Evaluate
As students draft, have them evaluate their work using the rubric on p. 104.

 Digital • eBook
• WriteSmart
• Interactive Lessons

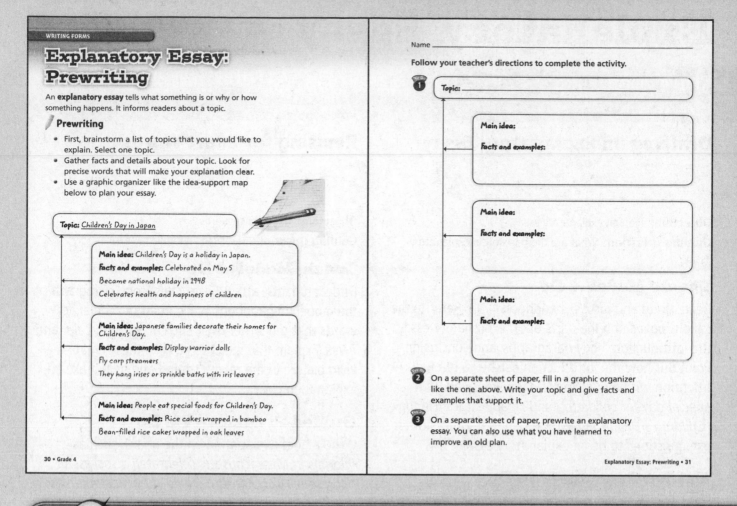

Explanatory Essay: Prewriting

An **explanatory essay** tells what something is or why or how something happens. It informs readers about a topic.

Prewriting

- First, brainstorm a list of topics that you would like to explain. Select one topic.
- Gather facts and details about your topic. Look for precise words that will make your explanation clear.
- Use a graphic organizer like the idea-support map below to plan your essay.

Topic: Children's Day in Japan

Main idea: Children's Day is a holiday in Japan.
Facts and examples: Celebrated on May 5
Became national holiday in 1948
Celebrates health and happiness of children

Main idea: Japanese families decorate their homes for Children's Day.
Facts and examples: Display warrior dolls
Fly carp streamers
They hang irises or sprinkle baths with iris leaves

Main idea: People eat special foods for Children's Day.
Facts and examples: Rice cakes wrapped in bamboo
Bean-filled rice cakes wrapped in oak leaves

Name _____

Follow your teacher's directions to complete the activity.

1 Topic: _____

Main idea:
Facts and examples:

Main idea:
Facts and examples:

Main idea:
Facts and examples:

2 On a separate sheet of paper, fill in a graphic organizer like the one above. Write your topic and give facts and examples that support it.

3 On a separate sheet of paper, prewrite an explanatory essay. You can also use what you have learned to improve an old plan.

Corrective Feedback

IF . . . students find it difficult to organize their explanatory essays,

THEN . . . have them try several different patterns to figure out which one works best. They might want to use their notes to make several idea-support maps before they begin to write. Remind them to group related facts and details together.

Focus Trait: Organization

Tell students that, in a good explanatory essay, a writer uses a pattern of organization that helps readers understand the topic. Remind students that an idea-support map can be especially helpful when writers need to organize information in a logical way.

Write these different patterns of organization on the board:

Tell what happened in sequence (time order)

Tell why something happened (cause/effect)

Tell about the parts that make up a whole (analysis)

Tell how things are alike or different (compare/contrast)

Discuss each pattern of organization. Then have students identify which pattern of organization the idea-support map on p. 30 uses *(tell about the parts that make up a whole).*

Explanatory Essay

Drafting an Explanatory Essay

Objective: Plan an explanatory essay.

Guiding Question: What are the parts of an explanatory essay?

Teach/Model—I Do

Read aloud and discuss handbook p. 32. Refer to the callout boxes and the parts of an explanatory essay: the introduction, body paragraphs, and conclusion. Point out how the introduction catches a reader's attention with a question (*Do you know about a special day for children?*) and clearly states the topic, (*Children's Day in Japan*). Explain that writers often use questions to begin explanatory essays.

Guided Practice—We Do

1 Direct students to the frame on handbook p. 33. Have them use their plans from Minilesson 18 about a holiday. Ask students to supply facts and examples to explain this topic. Together, complete the frame, including all the parts of an explanatory essay. Have students write in their books as you write on the board.

Practice/Apply—You Do

2 **COLLABORATIVE** Have groups plan and complete Activity 2. They may use their prewriting plans from Minilesson 18. Encourage them to think of facts and examples that will help readers understand this holiday.

3 **INDEPENDENT** Have students read and follow directions for Activity 3. Tell them to use their prewriting plan from Minilesson 18 or make another plan using Graphic Organizer 7.

Conference/Evaluate

As students draft, have them evaluate their work using the rubric on p. 104.

Revising for Exact Words

Objective: Use precise words.

Guiding Question: How can I improve my explanatory essay?

Teach/Model—I Do

Direct students' attention to the second paragraph of the model on handbook p. 32. Point out the exact words that the writer uses, such as *warrior*, *carp*, and *irises*. Explain that exact words like these create a vivid picture in the reader's mind and help make an explanation clear.

Guided Practice—We Do

Write a brief explanation on the board, such as *Pilgrims in Massachusetts celebrated a successful harvest in 1621. For three days, they feasted on deer, corn, clams, oysters, and roast duck. Today, most people enjoy delicious things on Thanksgiving.* Work with students to identify exact words that help readers understand the explanation. *(Pilgrims, Massachusetts, deer, and so on)* Ask: *How could we change the last sentence so that it has exact words?* (Sample answer: *Today, many Americans enjoy delicious turkey, cranberry sauce, and pumpkin pie on Thanksgiving.*)

Practice/Apply—You Do

COLLABORATIVE Have groups look over their drafts from Minilesson 19 to suggest places where they could substitute more exact words.

INDEPENDENT Have students revise their drafts from Minilesson 19. If they have used enough exact words, encourage them to look for places where they can replace a word they have used too often.

Conference/Evaluate

Have students review their revised drafts to make sure the drafts include exact words.

Digital
- eBook
- WriteSmart
- Interactive Lessons

Explanatory Essay

An **explanatory essay** explains a topic. It can tell what something is or why or how something happens. The purpose of an explanatory essay is to inform readers.

Parts of an Explanatory Essay

- An interesting introduction that tells about the topic
- Body paragraphs that each tell about one main idea
- Use of precise words that make the explanation clear
- Facts and examples that support main ideas about the topic
- An conclusion that ends the essay

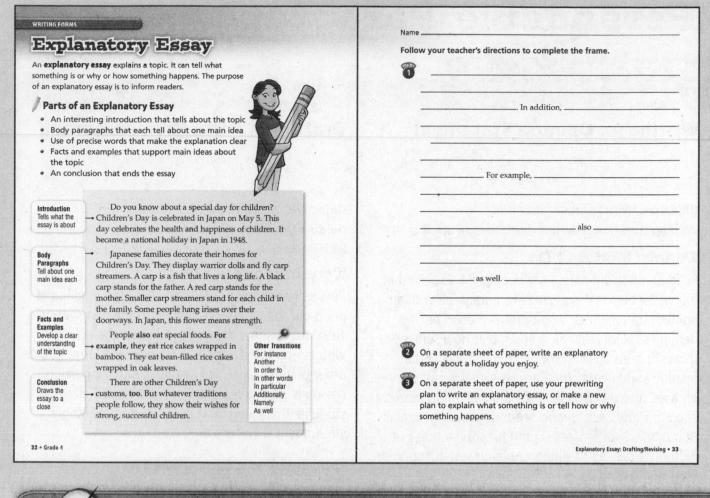

Introduction Tells what the essay is about	Do you know about a special day for children? Children's Day is celebrated in Japan on May 5. This day celebrates the health and happiness of children. It became a national holiday in Japan in 1948.
Body Paragraphs Tell about one main idea each	Japanese families decorate their homes for Children's Day. They display warrior dolls and fly carp streamers. A carp is a fish that lives a long life. A black carp stands for the father. A red carp stands for the mother. Smaller carp streamers stand for each child in the family. Some people hang irises over their doorways. In Japan, this flower means strength.
Facts and Examples Develop a clear understanding of the topic	People **also** eat special foods. **For example**, they eat rice cakes wrapped in bamboo. They eat bean-filled rice cakes wrapped in oak leaves.
Conclusion Draws the essay to a close	There are other Children's Day customs, **too**. But whatever traditions people follow, they show their wishes for strong, successful children.

Other Transitions
For instance
Another
In order to
In other words
In particular
Additionally
Namely
As well

Name _____

Follow your teacher's directions to complete the frame.

1

_____

_____ In addition, _____

_____

_____ For example, _____

_____

_____ also _____

_____

_____ as well. _____

_____

2 On a separate sheet of paper, write an explanatory essay about a holiday you enjoy.

3 On a separate sheet of paper, use your prewriting plan to write an explanatory essay, or make a new plan to explain what something is or tell how or why something happens.

Corrective Feedback

IF . . . students have trouble organizing their explanatory essays,

THEN . . . have them review each paragraph and cross out any sentences that do not tell something about the main idea of that paragraph.

Focus Trait: Elaboration

Tell students that, in a good explanatory essay, a writer elaborates by using precise, vivid words so that readers understand the explanation. Point out that exact words in the model, such as rice cakes and bamboo, provide the reader with important details about how people in Japan celebrate Children's Day.

Write this sentence on the board:

Flowers and candy are traditional Valentine's Day gifts.

Ask *Which words are most precise?* Elicit the words *traditional, Valentine's Day,* and *gifts.* Ask *Which words are not precise?* Elicit the words *flowers* and *candy.*

Have students suggest exact words that could replace *flowers* and *candy.* Help students understand that writers could make the sentence clearer by replacing vague words with more specific ones, such as *roses* and *chocolates.*

Persuasive Paragraph

Minilesson 21

Writing an Opinion Statement

Objective: Write an opinion statement.

Guiding Question: How do I clearly state my opinion?

Teach/Model—I Do

Read aloud and discuss handbook p. 34. Explain that the writer begins this persuasive paragraph with an opinion statement: *A rabbit makes a good pet.* Remind students that an opinion tells how someone thinks or feels about something. Tell students that opinion statements often include signal words or phrases such as *I believe, I think, I feel, in my opinion, should, should not, might, seem,* or *probably.* Explain that opinion statements cannot be proven true, but writers usually try to support opinion statements with facts and reasons.

Guided Practice—We Do

On the board, write these sentences:

(1) *Vegetables provide vitamins, minerals, and fiber.*

(2) *Kids should eat more vegetables.*

Work with students to identify the second sentence as an opinion statement. Help them understand that the word *should* signals an opinion.

Practice/Apply—You Do

COLLABORATIVE Write this sentence on the board: *Recycling is a way to reduce waste.* Have groups turn this sentence into a clear opinion statement by adding signal words or phrases.

INDEPENDENT Have students write an opinion statement about their favorite food.

Conference/Evaluate

Have students evaluate their statements to make sure they clearly state an opinion that can be supported with facts and reasons.

Minilesson 22

Drafting a Persuasive Paragraph

Objective: Write a paragraph to persuade readers.

Guiding Question: What facts, reasons, and examples support my opinion?

Teach/Model—I Do

Review handbook p. 34. Read aloud the model and point out the opinion statement in the first sentence. Then discuss how the writer supports the opinion with strong facts, reasons, and examples arranged in order of importance. For example, one supporting reason is *rabbits make only a little noise.* Tell students that using facts, reasons, and examples strengthens a writer's argument.

Guided Practice—We Do

 Direct students to the frame on handbook p. 35. Tell students that, together, you will write a persuasive paragraph about another animal that makes a good pet. Work with students to write an opinion statement. Then, together, complete the frame with facts, reasons, and examples that support the opinion. Have students write in their books as you write on the board.

Practice/Apply—You Do

 COLLABORATIVE Have groups plan and complete Activity 2. Have students look at local newspapers and websites for ideas. Have groups share what they have written.

INDEPENDENT Have students read and follow the directions. Tell them to use their prewriting plan from Lesson 11 or brainstorm a new plan. Have them use Graphic Organizer 15.

Conference/Evaluate

As students draft, have them evaluate their work using the rubric on p. 104.

Digital
• eBook
• WriteSmart
• Interactive Lessons

Persuasive Paragraph

A **persuasive paragraph** tries to convince readers to act or think in a certain way. It tells the writer's belief about a topic or an issue.

Parts of a Persuasive Paragraph

- A topic sentence that states the writer's opinion
- Facts, reasons, and examples that support the writer's opinion
- Reasons that are organized in order of importance
- Persuasive words and phrases to convince the reader

Topic Sentence
Tell how you feel about a subject

Supporting Details
Include strong facts, reasons, and examples

Organization
List the most important reason first or last

Persuasive Language
Use words like *popular* or *wonderful* to convince the reader

A rabbit makes a good pet. **First of all**, rabbits are clean. They spend a lot of time grooming their fur, and they can be trained to use a litter box like cats do. **Second**, rabbits are playful. They play with toys just as dogs and cats do, and they will run or hop around the house for exercise. **Third**, rabbits make only a little noise. Unlike dogs, rabbits don't bark. They only quietly grunt or stamp their feet when they are angry or upset. **Also**, rabbits like to be with people. To show their affection, they will lick or nibble you. **Most of all**, rabbits are intelligent and can be trained to do tricks, obey simple commands, and come when you call them. Pet rabbits have become more popular than ever. In 2007, there were more than 6 million pet rabbits in the United States. Are you thinking of getting a pet? Having a pet rabbit is a wonderful experience.

Other Transitions
Above all
Next
Last
Most importantly
Mainly
In addition
Most significant
Least Important

Name _____

Follow your teacher's directions to complete the frame.

1 I believe that _____
_____

First, _____
_____

_____ Second, _____

Third, _____
_____

_____ In addition, _____
_____

_____ Most importantly, _____
_____

2 On a separate sheet of paper, write a persuasive paragraph about an issue in your community that is important to you.

3 On a separate sheet of paper, use your prewriting plan to write a persuasive paragraph, or make a new plan to write about a change you believe must take place in your school.

Corrective Feedback

IF . . . students are having a hard time thinking of facts, reasons, and examples to support their opinions,

THEN . . . have them find additional information about this topic. They can consult websites, current magazines and newspapers, and reference books in the school library.

Focus Trait: Evidence

Tell students that, in a good persuasive paragraph, a writer uses evidence such as specific details to share ideas that support an opinion. Point out this sentence in the model:

They spend a lot of time grooming their fur, and they can be trained to use a litter box like a cat does.

Explain that these details help readers understand why rabbits are clean. They also help support the writer's opinion that rabbits make good pets.

Write this sentence on the board:

Saturday is the most enjoyable day of the week.

Have students list details and evidence and reasons that support the statement.

Problem-Solution Composition

Minilesson 23

Using Words that Persuade

Objective: Choose words to persuade the audience.

Guiding Question: What words will convince my readers?

Teach/Model—I Do

With students, read and discuss Parts of a Problem-Solution Composition on handbook p. 36. Point to the first paragraph of the model. Explain that the writer uses words that sound strong and forceful, such as *Something has to change!* Explain that the words writers use can help persuade their readers to understand a problem and to agree with the solution the writer suggests. Remind students that transition words link their opinions with reasons.

Guided Practice—We Do

Work with students to plan a problem-solution composition about crowded bus routes to school. Help students identify words or phrases that describe the problem. Then help them identify solutions (such as more buses) using persuasive words to help convince their readers. Write their suggestions on chart paper for use with Minilesson 24.

Practice/Apply—You Do

COLLABORATIVE Tell students to plan a problem-solution composition about a problem with your school's library, music room, or gym. Have pairs list words to convince their audience that the problem is important and their solution is good. Have groups save their notes.

INDEPENDENT Tell students to plan a problem-solution composition about a problem in their community. Have students write convincing words or phrases describing the problem and the solution.

Conference/Evaluate

If students are having trouble, suggest that they describe the problem aloud to partners.

Minilesson 24

Drafting a Problem-Solution Composition

Objective: Write a convincing problem-solution composition.

Guiding Question: How can I convince my audience that my solution is best?

Teach/Model—I Do

With students, review handbook p. 36. Read aloud the model, pointing out the problem and possible solutions. Explain that the last paragraph is a conclusion that presents the best solution.

Guided Practice—We Do

We Do 1 Have students turn to the frame on handbook p. 37. Using the ideas the class generated about bus routes in Minilesson 23, work together to put the problem and solutions into sentences. Guide students to pick the best solution to put in the concluding sentence. Have them write in their books as you write on the board.

Practice/Apply—You Do

You Do 2 **COLLABORATIVE** Have small groups plan and complete Activity 2. They can use their notes from Minilesson 23 or choose a new problem and identify at least one solution. Have groups share and discuss their writing.

You Do 3 **INDEPENDENT** Have students read the directions. Tell them to use their prewriting plan from Lesson 12 or brainstorm a new plan using Graphic Organizer 7.

Conference/Evaluate

Circulate and help students choose reasonable solutions. Evaluate using the rubric on p. 104.

 Digital
- eBook
- WriteSmart
- Interactive Lessons

Problem-Solution Composition

A **problem-solution composition** presents a problem and tells ways to solve it.

Parts of a Problem-Solution Composition

- An introduction that presents the problem
- A body that offers possible reasons and examples
- Language to persuade your audience
- A conclusion that tells the best solution

Introduction
Presents the problem

We students do not have time to eat lunch, even though we get a whole hour. It should be enough time, but it never is! The lunch lines are so long that they often take thirty minutes to get through! Then we have to gulp down our food and race back to class. Something has to change!

Solutions
Suggest ideas for fixing the problem

One way to improve things might be to stagger lunch. First, one class would go. Then, fifteen minutes later, the next class would follow, and so on. The lines would be shorter, and we

Reasons and Examples
Tell how the solutions work

would spend more time eating and less time waiting. **A second** way would be to hire another cashier and add another line. With two checkout lines, we could sit down to eat a lot faster.

Other Transitions
Next
Because
As a result
Finally
In addition
For instance
In order to

Conclusion
Names the best solution and gives reasons why it is best

Clearly, **the best solution** would be to stagger lunch. No more workers would be needed, and there would not be a need to buy another cash register. The school would just stagger the schedule. That way, we would make the most of our lunch time!

Name _____

Follow your teacher's directions to complete the frame.

1 One problem we have at school is _____

_____

One way _____

_____

A second way _____

_____

The best solution _____

_____

2 On a separate sheet of paper, plan and write a problem-solution composition about a problem with your school's library, music room, or gym. Suggest at least one possible solution.

3 On a separate sheet of paper, use your prewriting plan to write a problem-solution composition, or plan and write a composition about a problem in your community.

Corrective Feedback

IF . . . students are unable to come up with at least two reasonable solutions to their problem,

THEN . . . have them brainstorm ideas with partners or small groups. They can use other ideas that come up to prompt their own thinking. Students should record their preferred solutions in a web or other graphic organizer and provide reasons and facts or examples to support each solution.

Focus Trait: Evidence

Tell students that a strong problem-solution composition contains evidence that explains how the solution could be helpful. Good writers add details and other forms of evidence that help readers clearly understand why the solution will work.

Write *A student leader will help the school.* Explain that adding details could tell what kind of leader is needed and explain how he or she will help the school.

Write *Electing a student body president will help the school run smoothly because he or she can help the teachers and principal plan events, such as dances and book fairs.* Have students find vague ideas in their compositions and add evidence that will help show how the problem is solved.

Persuasive Letter

Minilesson 25

Using Business Letter Format

Objective: Use the correct format for a business letter.
Guiding Question: What are the parts of a business letter?

Teach/Model—I Do

Read aloud and discuss handbook p. 38. Explain that the writer, Matt Lucci, uses the correct format for a business letter. Discuss the parts of a business letter while having students examine each part in the model: the sender's address and the date; the receiver's name and address; the greeting that begins with *Dear* and ends with a comma; the body that states the purpose of the letter along with facts and details; the closing followed by a comma; and the writer's signature.

Guided Practice—We Do

On the board, write these parts of a business letter: (1) *Marie Amis* (2) *Dear Miss Evans,* (3) *Sincerely,* (4) *6 Main Street, Lauderhill, FL 33311* (5) *March 11, 2012.* (6) *Lauderhill should have a dog park. People need a place to take their dogs. I hope you will turn the old hospital grounds into a park. Then our dogs will be able to run and play off the leash.*

Work with students to put these parts in the correct format for a business letter.

Practice/Apply—You Do

COLLABORATIVE Direct groups to write a short business letter. Have them identify and label each of the six parts of the letter.

INDEPENDENT Have students write a business letter on their own, using correct format.

Conference/Evaluate

Have students share their business letters with you to make sure they have used the proper format.

Minilesson 26

Drafting a Persuasive Letter

Objective: Write a letter to persuade readers.
Guiding Question: What facts, reasons, and examples support the main points of my letter?

Teach/Model—I Do

Review handbook p. 38. Read aloud the model and point out how the writer supports his opinion that the skate park needs to be repaired. He backs up his opinion with strong facts, reasons, and examples. For example, Matt says *storms caused large cracks in the concrete bowl.* Explain that using specific details strengthens a writer's argument.

Guided Practice—We Do

We Do 1 Direct students to the frame on handbook p. 39. Tell students that together you will write a persuasive letter to the principal about an issue at school. For example, you might write about why your cafeteria should improve its menu. Work with students to complete the frame with facts, reasons, and examples that support the opinion. Have students write in their books as you write on the board.

Practice/Apply—You Do

You Do 2 **COLLABORATIVE** Have groups plan and complete Activity 2. To get them started, provide them with examples of letters to the editor from local newspapers. Have groups share what they have written.

You Do 3 **INDEPENDENT** Have students read and follow the directions. Tell them to use their prewriting plan from Lesson 13 or to brainstorm a new plan using Graphic Organizer 15.

Conference/Evaluate

As students draft, have them evaluate their work using the rubric on p. 104.

 Digital
- eBook
- WriteSmart
- Interactive Lessons

Persuasive Letter

A **persuasive letter** is a letter that is written to convince the reader to do something specific.

Parts of a Persuasive Letter

- A beginning that states the purpose for the letter
- Facts, reasons, and examples that support the main points of the letter
- A friendly, sincere tone
- The six parts of a letter: sender's address, date, recipient's address, body, closing, and signature

110 Fair Street
Brooksville, FL 34601
December 15, 2012

Mayor Jackson Murphy
206 Front Street
Brooksville, FL 34601

Dear Mayor Murphy,

Beginning
Asks the reader to do something

Details
Give specific facts, reasons, and examples

Tone
Sounds honest and positive

Building Brooksville Skate Park was a great idea. **However**, the park is now in bad shape, and the town must fix it. **For example**, the main gate sags. **Also**, a few of the ramps have rusty nails sticking out. **In addition**, storms caused large cracks in the concrete bowl. As a regular skateboarder, I feel the park is dangerous. Skaters can lose control and fall off their boards. **For this reason**, I hope you'll briefly close the park for repairs and help make us kids safer.

Sincerely,

Matt Lucci

Other Transitions
Because
On the other hand
Nevertheless
For instance
In order to
Although
In fact
Therefore

Name _____

Follow your teacher's directions to complete the frame.

1
_____
_____
_____

_____
_____
_____

Dear _____,

_____ because _____
_____

For instance, _____
_____ Also, _____
_____ Finally, _____

For this reason, _____
_____

Sincerely,
_____

2 On a separate sheet of paper, write a persuasive letter to the editor of your local newspaper. It should be about a situation that you feel strongly about.

3 On a separate sheet of paper, use your prewriting plan to write a persuasive letter, or make a new plan to write a persuasive letter in which you make a specific request.

Corrective Feedback

IF . . . students are having a hard time thinking of facts, reasons, and examples to support the main points of the letter,

THEN . . . have them use websites, current magazines and newspapers, and other resources in the school library to find information about this topic.

Focus Trait: Purpose

Tell students that in a good persuasive letter, a writer sets a sincere tone that the reader can trust. The writer does this by keeping the purpose for writing in mind, and choosing the right words. Explain that some words can elicit a strong positive or negative emotional reaction.

In the model, for example, Matt says *I hope you'll briefly close the park for repairs and help make us kids safer.* Point out how specific words like *I hope* and *us kids* make the writer's voice sound friendly and sincere.

Write these sentences on the board:

You'd better send money right now to Save Our Pets.

Please consider giving today to Save Our Pets.

Guide students to understand that the first sentence uses a threatening tone and harsh language. In contrast, the second sentence is written in a polite, friendly way.

Persuasive Essay: Prewriting

Persuading an Audience to Take Action

Objective: Use strong facts and examples.

Guiding Question: How can I convince my audience to do something?

Teach/Model—I Do

Read aloud and discuss handbook p. 40. Ask *What is the writer's goal?* (To start a worm farm at school.) Help students understand how the writer persuades readers to support the worm farm. Point out that, in the idea-support map, the writer gives strong facts and examples to support each reason. Explain that strong facts and examples will help convince readers to take action.

Guided Practice—We Do

On the board, write a two-column chart with these headings: *Facts* and *Examples*. Direct students to the idea-support map and help them identify facts *(Two pounds of worms can eat a whole pound of fruits and vegetables and other waste)* and examples *(There would be less garbage for the school to send to the landfill)*. Tell students that these strong facts and examples support each reason.

Practice/Apply—You Do

COLLABORATIVE Have groups choose a topic that they feel strongly about. Then have them list facts and examples that support their opinion.

INDEPENDENT Have students choose another topic they feel strongly about and list facts and examples that would persuade an audience to take action.

Conference/Evaluate

Have students look over their lists of facts and examples to make sure they are persuasive.

Organizing a Persuasive Essay

Objective: Determine how to organize a persuasive essay.

Guiding Question: How should I arrange my essay?

Teach/Model—I Do

Review handbook p. 40. Explain to students that filling out an idea-support map can help them draft persuasive essays. Point out the reason and supporting facts and examples in each box of the idea-support map. Tell students that a good persuasive essay is organized in a way that will best persuade readers to agree with a writer's opinion.

Guided Practice—We Do

We Do 1 Direct students to Activity 1 on handbook p. 41. Work with students to choose a topic, such as something the school could do to improve the environment. Then, together, complete the frame with reasons, facts, and examples that support the opinion. Have students write in their books as you write on the board.

Practice/Apply—You Do

You Do 2 **COLLABORATIVE** Have groups plan and complete Activity 2. Have them choose an opinion about something your town or community should do and create an idea-support map together. Then have groups share what they have written.

You Do 3 **INDEPENDENT** Have students read and follow the directions. Tell them to use their prewriting plan from Lesson 14 or to brainstorm a new plan using Graphic Organizer 7.

Conference/Evaluate

As students draft, have them evaluate their work using the rubric on p. 104.

Digital
• eBook
• WriteSmart
• Interactive Lessons

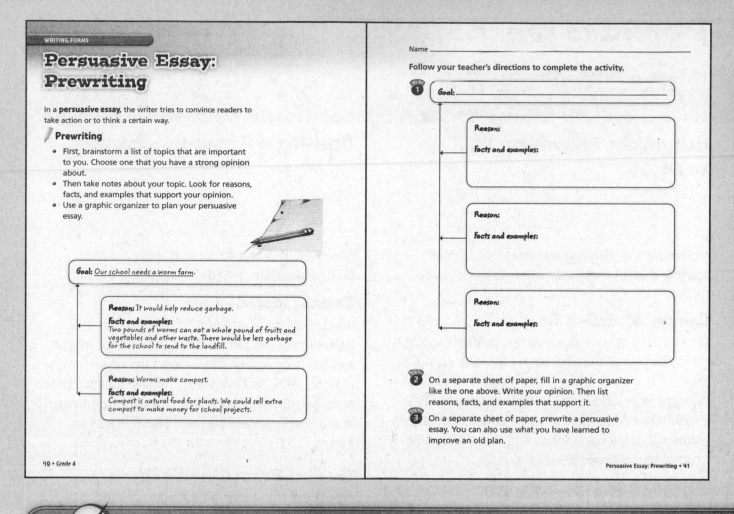

Persuasive Essay: Prewriting

In a **persuasive essay**, the writer tries to convince readers to take action or to think a certain way.

✏ Prewriting

- First, brainstorm a list of topics that are important to you. Choose one that you have a strong opinion about.
- Then take notes about your topic. Look for reasons, facts, and examples that support your opinion.
- Use a graphic organizer to plan your persuasive essay.

Goal: Our school needs a worm farm.

Reason: It would help reduce garbage.
Facts and examples:
Two pounds of worms can eat a whole pound of fruits and vegetables and other waste. There would be less garbage for the school to send to the landfill.

Reason: Worms make compost.
Facts and examples:
Compost is natural food for plants. We could sell extra compost to make money for school projects.

Name _____

Follow your teacher's directions to complete the activity.

1 Goal: _____

Reason:
Facts and examples:

Reason:
Facts and examples:

Reason:
Facts and examples:

2 On a separate sheet of paper, fill in a graphic organizer like the one above. Write your opinion. Then list reasons, facts, and examples that support it.

3 On a separate sheet of paper, prewrite a persuasive essay. You can also use what you have learned to improve an old plan.

✓ Corrective Feedback

IF . . . students find it hard to think of facts and examples that will persuade readers,

THEN . . . have them look for additional information related to their topics. Suggest that they consult magazines, newspapers, reference books, and news websites for ideas.

Focus Trait: Organization

Tell students that writers organize ideas in a way that persuades readers to agree with the writer's opinion. Explain that the most important reason should come last, right before the call to action, so that the reader feels convinced to take that action.

On the board, write the following topic: *Our school should grow a garden.*

Then write these reasons to support it.

(1) A school garden brings together students and adults in the community.

(2) School gardens encourage healthy eating.

(3) School gardens are attractive.

Help students organize the reasons from least to most important. (3, 1, 2)

Persuasive Essay

Minilesson 29

Using Your Prewriting Plan to Draft

Objective: Use an idea-support map to write a draft.

Guiding Question: How do I turn my prewriting into a persuasive essay?

Teach/Model—I Do

Direct students back to handbook p. 40 and point out the opinion in the idea-support map: *Our school needs a worm farm.* Then have students look at the reasons, facts, and examples that the writer lists. Explain that the writer states clear ideas and arranges them in a logical order so that this plan can be used to write a good persuasive essay.

Guided Practice—We Do

Work with students to turn information in the first box of the idea-support map on handbook p. 41 into a paragraph. Ask questions, such as *What is the main idea?* and *What are the supporting sentences?* Write students' suggestions on the board, work with them to choose the best ones, and then guide them to suggest transitions to connect their sentences.

Practice/Apply—You Do

COLLABORATIVE Have groups write a paragraph based on information in the second box of the idea-support map on handbook p. 41.

INDEPENDENT Have students revise their own idea-support maps. Remind them to state ideas clearly and arrange them logically, removing unnecessary ideas and moving ones that are out of order.

Conference/Evaluate

Have students share their prewriting plans to check that they are complete and accurate.

Minilesson 30

Drafting a Persuasive Essay

Objective: Plan a persuasive essay.

Guiding Question: How do I write a persuasive essay?

Teach/Model—I Do

Read aloud handbook p. 42. Point out that the beginning of this model states the writer's opinion and the body paragraphs support the opinion with reasons, facts, and examples. Remind students that a good persuasive essay has strong reasons arranged in order of importance as well as a final call to action.

Guided Practice—We Do

 Direct students to the frame on handbook p. 43. Tell them that, together, you will write a persuasive essay about how your school can help reduce energy costs by turning off lights when not in use, replacing regular light bulbs, and so on. Then, together, complete the frame using your prewriting plans from Minilessons 28 and 29 as a guide. Have students write in their books as you write on the board.

Practice/Apply—You Do

 COLLABORATIVE Have groups plan and complete Activity 2. They can use their prewriting plans from Minilesson 28 as a guide.

INDEPENDENT Have students read and follow the directions for Activity 3. Tell them to use their prewriting plan from Lesson 15 or to make a new plan using Graphic Organizer 7.

Conference/Evaluate

As students draft, have them evaluate their work using the rubric on p. 104.

Digital
- eBook
- WriteSmart
- Interactive Lessons

Persuasive Essay

A **persuasive essay** tries to convince readers to do something or to think a certain way.

Parts of a Persuasive Essay
- A beginning that grabs readers' interest
- A clear statement of the writer's opinion
- Reasons, facts, and examples that support the writer's opinion
- An ending that tells readers what to do

Beginning Makes readers want to learn more

Opinion States what the writer believes

Reasons, Facts, and Examples Support the writer's opinion

Ending Tells readers what to do

You might think that worms are gross, but they are some of nature's most amazing recycling machines. That is why I believe our school needs a worm farm.

First, a worm farm would help us reduce the amount of garbage the school sends to the landfill. Each day, two pounds of worms can eat a whole pound of fruits, vegetables, and other garbage. Think of how much less garbage there would be to cart away!

Also, worms make compost. Compost is natural food for plants. We could sell any extra compost and make money for school projects.

In the end, a school worm farm is a winning idea. Come to the meeting Monday to vote YES for the worm farm.

Other Transitions
First of all
Second
Next
Finally
As a result
In addition

Name _____

Follow your teacher's directions to complete the frame.

1 To help the environment, our school _____

First, _____

Also, _____

In the end, _____

2 On a separate sheet of paper, write a persuasive essay about something the people in your town should do.

3 On a separate sheet of paper, use your prewriting plan to write a persuasive essay, or plan and write a new persuasive essay about something that is important to you.

Corrective Feedback

IF . . . students have difficulty using their idea-support maps to draft persuasive essays,

THEN . . . have them go back to their idea-support maps and look at their reasons and the facts and examples they used to back them up. Suggest that students review their research notes or do further research to find additional persuasive reasons, facts, and examples. Then have them revise their idea-support maps.

Focus Trait: Evidence

Tell students that good writers include evidence in a persuasive essay so that readers can more easily make sense of the writer's argument. Point out that in the model the writer's argument is built on sound reasons that are backed up with persuasive facts and examples. Explain that reasons, facts, and examples must make sense to readers or they won't be persuaded.

On the board, write the following opinion: *Our town should plant more trees to help the environment.*

Then write these reasons on the board:

Trees are fun to play in.

Trees produce oxygen.

Trees are nice to look at.

Have students choose the reason that best supports this opinion. *(Trees produce oxygen.)* Then help students suggest facts and examples that will support this reason.

Descriptive Paragraph

Using Vivid Words

Objective: Use vivid words to bring a subject to life.

Guiding Question: What details will create a picture in a reader's mind?

Teach/Model—I Do

Read aloud and discuss handbook p. 44. Explain that the writer uses vivid details to describe people, places, and events. On the board, write this sentence from the model: *Near the entrance, noisy children play on slippery metal slides, climbing ladders, and blue plastic swings*. Point out that *slippery* tells how the slides feel and *metal* tells what the slides look like. The words *blue* and *plastic* tell how the swings look and feel. Explain that these details help readers picture the park in their minds.

Guided Practice—We Do

On the board, create a five-column chart with these headings: *Sight, Touch, Sound, Smell, Taste*. Work with students to find details in the model paragraph that appeal to one or more of these senses. Then write these details in the appropriate columns of the chart. Guide students to discuss how these details bring Bailey Park to life.

Practice/Apply—You Do

COLLABORATIVE Have groups choose three objects in the school. Then direct them to make charts with the headings *Look, Feel, Sound, Smell, Taste*. Have groups fill in the chart with vivid details that describe this object.

INDEPENDENT Have students make a list of vivid details to describe the school lunchroom.

Conference/Evaluate

Have students review their lists to make sure they have come up with clear, strong details.

Drafting a Descriptive Paragraph

Objective: Write a paragraph that describes.

Guiding Question: How will I describe my subject?

Teach/Model—I Do

Review handbook p. 44. Read aloud the model and point out how the writer identifies the subject, *Bailey Park*, in the topic sentence. Remind students that the writer uses sensory details such as *long green pine needles* and exact words such as *marsh* or *reeds* to clearly describe the park. Point out how the writer wraps up the description in the ending.

Guided Practice—We Do

We Do 1 Direct students to the frame on handbook p. 45. Tell students that you will write a descriptive paragraph about a familiar place. Work with students to brainstorm a topic, such as your classroom or a favorite store. Then, together, complete the frame with vivid details and exact words. Have students write in their books as you write on the board.

Practice/Apply—You Do

You Do 2 **COLLABORATIVE** Have groups plan and complete Activity 2. Encourage them to write about a well-known celebrity or community leader. Have groups share what they have written.

You Do 3 **INDEPENDENT** Have students read and follow the directions. Tell them to use their prewriting plan from Lesson 16 or to brainstorm a new plan using Graphic Organizer 15.

Conference/Evaluate

As students draft, have them evaluate their work using the rubric on p. 104.

 Digital
• eBook
• WriteSmart
• Interactive Lessons

Descriptive Paragraph

A **descriptive paragraph** describes, or tells about, a person, place, thing, or event. A descriptive paragraph helps create a picture in the reader's mind.

Parts of a Descriptive Paragraph

- A topic sentence that tells the subject of the paragraph
- Vivid details that clearly describe a person, place, thing, or event
- Strong words that help readers picture what is being described
- An ending that wraps up the description

Topic Sentence
Tells what the paragraph is about

Sensory Details
Tell how the subject looks, feels, sounds, smells, or tastes

Exact Words
Include specific nouns, verbs, and adjectives

Ending
Sums up the paragraph

Bailey Park is a great place to visit! A snack bar **next to** the parking lot sells yummy ice cream, cold drinks, popcorn, and other food. **Near** the entrance, noisy children play on slippery metal slides, climbing ladders, and blue plastic swings. Older kids race around the grassy soccer fields **behind** the swings. They also use the lighted basketball and tennis courts. There is a small picnic area **in the middle** of the park. You can eat your lunch **under** towering pine trees. Long green pine needles on the ground **by** the picnic tables feel as soft as a rug. Dad and I like to take the hiking trail **around** the marsh. It's a winding dirt path, which is marked with bright yellow triangles so you don't get lost. Sometimes, I hear frogs croaking in the reeds. Dad looks for interesting birds with his field glasses. Bailey Park has something for people of all ages.

Other Transitions
Above
Across
Below
Beside
Inside
Outside
At the bottom
Beyond

Name _____

Follow your teacher's directions to complete the frame.

1 A place I know well is _____

Near _____

Next to _____

_____ . Behind _____

Under _____

_____ in the middle of _____

_____ Above _____

2 On a separate sheet of paper, write a descriptive paragraph about a person you know well.

3 On a separate sheet of paper, use your prewriting plan to write a descriptive paragraph, or make a new plan to write about a familiar object in your room at home.

Corrective Feedback

IF . . . students are having a hard time coming up with vivid details and exact words to describe their subject,

THEN . . . have them close their eyes and visualize the subject. Tell them to jot down words that describe what they might see, feel, hear, smell, or taste.

Focus Trait: Elaboration

Explain that in a descriptive paragraph, good writers include vivid details that can help the reader picture what is being described. In the model, for example, the writer says *Long green pine needles on the ground by the picnic tables feel as soft as a rug.* Point out that these kinds of details help convey what Bailey Park is like.

Write these sentences on the board:

Joe's Deli is dirty and crowded.

Joe's Deli is crammed with sagging wooden shelves packed with dusty cans.

Guide students to understand that the first sentence describes what Joe's Deli is like, but adding vivid details to the second sentence really makes it come alive. Ask *Which details in the second sentence help the reader picture the deli?* Elicit the words *crammed, wooden, sagging, packed,* and *dusty.*

Friendly Letter

Matching Words with Audience

Objective: Select specific words and phrases for audience.

Guiding Question: How will my words affect my audience?

Teach/Model—I Do

Read and discuss handbook p. 46. Tell students that, when writing a letter, they should consider the recipient and the effect their words will have on that person. A letter to a friend or relative might be informal or friendly. A letter to a newspaper might be more formal. Explain that sentences in the model like *I was so excited* and *I'd love to see you* are informal and express the writer's feelings. Also note that these sentences will make Jenny's aunt feel good.

Guided Practice—We Do

On the board, write *You haven't been at school.* Work with students to make this sentence to a sick friend more personal. Explain that they can use informal words since the letter is to a friend and that they should think of things to say that would make the friend feel better, such as *I can't wait until you're back!* Write students' suggestions on the board.

Practice/Apply—You Do

COLLABORATIVE Have students imagine that they are writing a letter to an adult relative who has won a tennis tournament. On the board, write *I heard about the game.* Have groups write some words and phrases that would convey their excitement and make the relative feel good.

INDEPENDENT Have students imagine that they are writing a letter to a classmate who has lost her favorite bracelet. On the board, write *It's too bad about your bracelet.* Have students rewrite the sentence to show their sympathy for the classmate.

Conference/Evaluate

Encourage students to list precise words to describe how they feel and what happened.

Drafting a Friendly Letter

Objective: Compose a friendly letter.

Guiding Question: How do I express my feelings and ideas in a friendly letter?

Teach/Model—I Do

With students, review handbook p. 46. Review the parts of the letter, including the address, date, greeting, closing, and signature. Draw students' attention to the commas used in the model. Remind them that the body of a friendly letter should have an informal, friendly voice. Go over the Closings box.

Guided Practice—We Do

 Direct students to the frame on handbook p. 47. Read the first line aloud. Have students suggest a recipient for the letter. Then help them plan details for the body of the letter. Guide students to suggest sentences to complete the frame. Have them write in their books as you write on the board.

Practice/Apply—You Do

 COLLABORATIVE Have small groups complete Activity 2. Tell them to choose a recipient, to decide on an event, to name it in the letter's opening sentence, and to include interesting details about it. Remind students to choose words with the recipient in mind.

INDEPENDENT Have students read the directions. Tell them to use their prewriting plan from Lesson 17 or to brainstorm a new plan. Tell them to use correct letter form.

Conference/Evaluate

As students draft, circulate and help them choose words appropriate for their audiences. Evaluate using the rubric on p. 104.

Digital
- eBook
- WriteSmart
- Interactive Lessons

Friendly Letter

A **friendly letter** is written to someone the writer knows well. It includes informal, familiar language.

Parts of a Friendly Letter

- The writer's address and the date
- A greeting to the person who will receive the letter
- A body that makes up the main part of the letter
- Interesting details about the topic
- An informal, friendly voice
- A closing and the writer's signature

Greeting
Tells whom the letter is to

Body
The main part of the letter

Friendly Voice
Sounds like the person speaking

Interesting Details
Keep the reader interested

Closing and Signature

27 Palmetto Road
St. Petersburg, FL 33784
March 12, 2013

Dear Aunt Camille,

    Did Mom tell you the big news? I landed the lead part in the class play! When I first saw flyers for it, I knew I wanted to try out. I was so scared during the tryout! There was a bunch of other girls who wanted a part, too. First, we had to stand up in front of our classmates and read a few lines. We also took turns singing. The next day, my teacher announced that I had the part! I was so excited. I like being an actor. Will you come for the play? I'd love to see you!

Your niece,
Jenny

Closings
Your friend
Sincerely
Best wishes
Love

Name _____

Follow your teacher's directions to complete the frame.

1
_____
_____
_____

Dear _____,

Did you hear the news? I won my soccer game last weekend! _____
_____
_____
_____
_____
_____
_____
_____

Sincerely,

_____

2 On a separate sheet of paper, plan and write a friendly letter to a friend or family member about something unusual that happened at school.

3 On a separate sheet of paper, use your prewriting plan to write a friendly letter, or plan and write a letter to a friend about something fun you did with your family.

Corrective Feedback

IF . . . students have difficulty choosing words to suit their audience,

THEN . . . have them consult a thesaurus and a dictionary to improve word choice. Tell them to make sure they check the definitions of unfamiliar synonyms before they use them in their writing.

Focus Trait: Purpose

Explain to students that when their writing purpose is to write a friendly letter, they can use informal language. The language will sound like the words they would say aloud. Tell students to take a few minutes to think about expressions they use when talking with friends.

If necessary, prompt students by asking *How do you greet your friends? What do you say when you are excited?* Have volunteers share expressions and then record them on the board. Tell students that, when they write their letters, they should recall their purpose and use familiar expressions to capture their own personalities on the page.

Using Imagery

Objective: Use imagery to describe.

Guiding Question: How can I use sensory details, vivid adjectives and active verbs to create strong mental images?

Teach/Model—I Do

Read aloud and discuss handbook p. 48. Explain that, in a story, descriptive words help readers form mental pictures of people, places, and events. Point to examples in the model, such as *like he had a bad cold* to describe how Juan sounded. Explain that Juan doesn't have a bad cold, but this specific image gives a clear idea of how he sounds. Point to other examples of descriptive words in the model or in classroom books. Discuss how these make the writing clear and interesting.

Guided Practice—We Do

On the board, write *The train conductor shouted.* Guide students to think about how they might make the sentence more descriptive, such as *The train conductor boomed like an elephant.*

Practice/Apply—You Do

COLLABORATIVE Write the following sentences on the board: *The bus stopped. The doors opened.* Have groups work together to add or change words or phrases to make the sentence more descriptive.

INDEPENDENT Have students choose two sentences from the model and use descriptive words to make them even more vivid.

Conference/Evaluate

Have students evaluate their sentences to make sure they have used descriptive words to make their stories come to life.

Drafting a Story

Objective: Write an interesting and engaging story.

Guiding Question: How can I keep my audience interested in the events and characters in my story?

Teach/Model—I Do

Review handbook p. 48. Point out that the first two sentences of the model tell readers about the character and the event. Explain that the descriptive words get and hold the reader's interest. Then point to the events in the story, discussing how the writer uses transition words to show the order of events.

Guided Practice—We Do

We Do 1 Direct students to the frame on handbook p. 49. Say that, together, you will write a story about a boy who wants to win a spelling bee. Guide students to write a first line, such as *Even though he knew his words well, Michael was really nervous about the spelling bee.* Together, complete the frame by adding imagery and writing the steps the boy took to win. Have students write in their books as you write on the board.

Practice/Apply—You Do

You Do 2 **COLLABORATIVE** Have pairs of students plan and complete Activity 2. Tell them to use descriptive words and sequence words. Have groups share what they have written.

You Do 3 **INDEPENDENT** Have students read and follow the directions. Tell them to use their prewriting plan from Lesson 18 or to brainstorm a new plan using Graphic Organizer 10.

Conference/Evaluate

As students draft, have them evaluate their work using the rubric on p. 104.

 Digital
- eBook
- WriteSmart
- Interactive Lessons

Story

A **story** describes either a real or an imaginary experience or event. A fictional story is imagined or made up by the writer.

Parts of a Story

- A beginning that grabs the reader's attention
- Events told in time order, or sequence
- Use of synonyms, or words with the same or nearly the same meanings, to keep the story interesting
- An ending that tells how the story worked out

Beginning
Starts with an interesting opening

Events
Tell what happened in time order

Synonyms
Keep the story from using the same words too often

Ending
Wraps up the story

Thunk. Juan dropped the heavy microphone, which made a screeching noise as it smashed on the floor. **Then** he waited awkwardly for the music to start, but the dark auditorium was silent. Juan coughed and stared at the ceiling. **After** a few long minutes, the judges instructed Juan to go ahead—without music.

At last, Juan tried to sing, but his throat had tightened up because he was nervous. He sounded hoarse, like he had a bad cold. **When** Juan finished, he stomped off the stage and glared at the other singers. He had blown any chance to win.

Lisa felt awful about Juan's disaster and told him about her worst flop. "Meltdowns happen, but you'll learn how to deal with them. Do you want to rehearse together for the contest next month?" she asked.

Juan and Lisa practiced every day **until** the next competition. In the end, they won first prize.

Other Transitions
First
Next
After that
During
After a while
Meanwhile
Later
Last

Name _____

Follow your teacher's directions to complete the frame.

1 _____
_____

At first, _____

_____ Then _____
_____
_____
_____ Next, _____
_____
_____
_____
_____ After that, _____
_____
_____ Finally, _____
_____
_____

2 On a separate sheet of paper, write a story about someone who makes a new a friend.

3 On a separate sheet of paper, use your prewriting plan to write a story, or make a new plan to write about a person who wins something.

✓ Corrective Feedback

IF ... students are having difficulty coming up with descriptive words and phrases,

THEN ... have them form pictures in their minds of how a character acts or talks or how an event unfolds. Ask questions such as *What does the audience look like or do when the boy wins the spelling bee? Clap politely? Jump up and cheer loudly?* Once they have an image in their minds, have students describe it as they have pictured it.

Focus Trait: Elaboration

Tell students that, when writing a story, one way to elaborate and find just the right word or phrase is to look in a thesaurus. Explain that a thesaurus is a book that lists words and gives synonyms, or words that are similar in meaning, for each word. Point out that thesauruses list words in alphabetical order, like dictionaries. In addition, word processing programs often include a thesaurus.

Model using a thesaurus to find a synonym for a less descriptive word, such as *look*. On the board, write some of the words you find, such as *gaze*, *stare*, *glare*, and *peek*. Discuss how one of these words might be a more descriptive choice than *look*, and how it might help to elaborate to add meaning and clarity. Give another word, such as *walk*, and have students practice looking up words and their synonyms.

Personal Narrative: Prewriting

Minilesson 37

Choosing an Interesting Event

Objective: Select an interesting true story.

Guiding Question: What story should I write about?

Teach/Model—I Do

Read aloud and discuss handbook p. 50. Point out the list of topic ideas that the writer brainstormed. Explain that the writer listed true stories: *giving food to a food bank, making a hummingbird feeder,* and *riding a horse at Windy Farm.* Tell students that the writer chose the first idea and then used the events chart to organize ideas and details.

Guided Practice—We Do

Work with students to brainstorm true stories about experiences your class has had, such as taking a field trip or listening to a guest speaker. Help students list suggestions on the board. Guide them to decide which experience would make the most interesting personal narrative. Have a volunteer put a star beside it.

Practice/Apply—You Do

COLLABORATIVE Have groups brainstorm a list of topics for true stories that happened to them. Have them select the topic that would be most interesting and that would have plenty of events and details to write about.

INDEPENDENT Have individuals brainstorm a list of topics for true stories and pick one that they would most like to write about. Remind students that they should be able to explain and justify their choices.

Conference/Evaluate

Remind students to consider whether their story has enough events and details to write about.

Minilesson 38

Planning a Personal Narrative

Objective: Plan a personal narrative.

Guiding Question: How will I tell about what happened?

Teach/Model—I Do

Review handbook p. 50. Point out the events chart. Ask *What is the first event? What details does the writer include?* Then discuss the events and details in the second and third sections. Help students understand that an events chart can outline events in the order in which they happened and that it also provides details about these events. Tell students that an events chart like this one can help them plan and organize their personal narratives.

Guided Practice—We Do

 1 Direct students to Activity 1 on handbook p. 51. Say that, together, you will create an events chart for the starred class story from Minilesson 37. Then, together, complete the chart with events and details that tell about this story. Have students write in their books as you write on the board.

Practice/Apply—You Do

2 **COLLABORATIVE** Have groups plan and complete Activity 2. Tell them to work together to create an events chart and then share their work with other groups.

3 **INDEPENDENT** Have students read and follow the directions. Tell them to use their prewriting plan from Lesson 19 or brainstorm a new plan using either Graphic Organizer 4 or an events chart.

Conference/Evaluate

As students draft, have them evaluate their work using the rubric on p. 104.

 Digital
- eBook
- WriteSmart
- Interactive Lessons

Personal Narrative: Prewriting

A **personal narrative** tells about something that happened to the writer and describes how the writer feels about the events.

Prewriting for Personal Narrative

- Brainstorm a list of true stories that happened to you.
- Pick one story that made a strong impression on you.
- Use a graphic organizer to plan your writing.

Topic Ideas

(Giving food to a food bank)

Making a hummingbird feeder

Riding a horse at Windy Farm

Event: My class wanted to give food to a food bank.

Details: My uncle is a chef. He offered to give us cooking lessons at his restaurant.

Event: Class met at my uncle's restaurant.

Details: We unpacked our cooking tools. My uncle showed us how to make different dishes. My group made pumpkin pie.

Event: We took the food to the food bank.

Details: Ms. Chao, the head of the food bank, thanked us. She said it would be the best Thanksgiving food a lot of people had. Everyone clapped for us. I felt great.

Name _____

Follow your teacher's directions to complete the activity.

1

Event:

Details:

Event:

Details:

Event:

Details:

2 On a separate sheet of paper, fill in a graphic organizer like the one above. Write your ideas for a personal narrative about something you did to help others.

3 On a separate sheet of paper, prewrite a personal narrative. You can also use what you have learned to improve an old plan.

Corrective Feedback

IF . . . students have difficulty thinking of details to include in their events charts,

THEN . . . have them ask themselves questions such as *Who? Where? What?* Explain that the answers to such questions help writers think of details that belong in their personal narratives.

Focus Trait: Organization

Tell students that writers organize their personal narratives in ways that help readers better understand the story. For example, writers often use time order to tell what happened since time order helps readers follow the story in the same order in which the events happened.

Explain that an events chart can help writers arrange the events and details of a personal narrative.

Write these sentences on the board:

(1) She showed us rough sketches for her new book.

(2) A children's book artist visited our class.

(3) We asked her questions about her sketches.

Have students explain how they would use an events chart to organize these events in time order (2, 1, 3). Elicit details they might add to the chart.

Personal Narrative

Minilesson 39

Keeping Readers Interested

Objective: Use details that will bring a narrative to life.

Guiding Question: How will I keep my readers interested?

Teach/Model—I Do

Read aloud and discuss handbook p. 52. Explain that the beginning of the model grabs the reader's interest with a question. Point out that the writer makes the story more interesting by including details about the experience and how people felt about it. Illustrate this by pointing out the descriptive details in the second paragraph: *My group made pumpkin pie.* Also, point out the dialogue at the end, which brings Ms. Chao and her feelings to life.

Guided Practice—We Do

Work with students to add interesting details to your events charts from Activity 1 on handbook p. 51. Ask *Which details will help readers picture what happened? Which details will help readers understand our feelings about what happened?* Have students write their ideas in their events charts as you write on the board.

Practice/Apply—You Do

COLLABORATIVE Have groups discuss their events charts from Activity 2 on handbook p. 51. Tell them to add descriptive details to their events charts. Remind them to include details about the experience and how people felt about it.

INDEPENDENT Have students brainstorm details and feelings about their events charts from Activity 3 on handbook p. 51. Have them add descriptive details to their events charts.

Conference/Evaluate

Have students share their revised charts with you to make sure they added appropriate details. Remind them that they can also add dialogue to bring feelings and experiences to life.

Minilesson 40

Drafting a Personal Narrative

Objective: Write a personal narrative.

Guiding Question: What will I tell readers about my experience?

Teach/Model—I Do

Review handbook p. 52. Refer to the callouts and have students identify the parts of a personal narrative: the *beginning, the events and details of the body paragraphs,* and the *ending.*

Guided Practice—We Do

 Direct students to the frame on handbook p. 53. Tell students that you will work together to write about a class experience. Have students complete the first sentence. Then, together, complete the frame with interesting events and details. Use your prewriting plan from handbook p. 51 as a guide. Have students write in their books as you write on the board.

Practice/Apply—You Do

 COLLABORATIVE Have groups plan and complete Activity 2. Encourage them to write about a class activity, such as a musical performance. Have groups share their work.

 INDEPENDENT Have students read and follow the directions. Tell them to use their prewriting plan from handbook p. 51 or to brainstorm a new plan using either Graphic Organizer 4 or an events chart.

Conference/Evaluate

Have students review their drafts to be sure they have told events in time order and included the kind of details that will keep readers interested.

Digital
• eBook
• WriteSmart
• Interactive Lessons

Personal Narrative

A **personal narrative** is a true story about something that happened to the writer. It tells how the writer feels about the events.

Parts of a Personal Narrative

- A beginning that grabs readers' interest
- Events that really happened to the writer, told in time order
- Interesting details about the events
- The writer's feelings about what happened

Beginning
Makes readers want to find out more

Have you ever wanted to be a chef? Everyone in my class got to be one this year. We wanted to donate food to a food bank. My uncle is a chef, and he offered to give us cooking lessons at his restaurant.

Events
Tell what happened in time order

To start, the class met at the restaurant and unpacked our tools. **Then** my uncle showed us how to make different dishes. My group made pumpkin pie. It was hard work, but it was worth it!

Interesting Details
Include sights, sounds, and feelings

Finally, we packed up the food and took it to the food bank. The head of the food bank, Ms. Chao, was waiting for us.

Ending
Tells how the writer felt

"This will be the best Thanksgiving food a lot of people have ever had! Thank you!" she said. **At the end,** everyone clapped for us, and I felt great.

Other Transitions
First
Second
During
After a while
Meanwhile
Later
Last

Name _____

Follow your teacher's directions to complete the frame.

1 I had an amazing time when our class went _____

_____

To start, _____

_____

_____ Then _____

_____

_____

_____

_____

_____

_____ Later, _____

_____

_____

_____ Last, _____

2 On a separate sheet of paper, write a personal narrative about one of the best things you ever did with your class.

3 On a separate sheet of paper, use your prewriting plan to write a personal narrative, or plan and write a new personal narrative about something you or your class did that helped other people.

Corrective Feedback

IF . . . students have difficulty organizing and drafting their personal narratives,

THEN . . . have them tell a classmate what happened so that, together, they can review events and come up with more details. Also remind students to use appropriate transitions to make the order of events clear.

Focus Trait: Development

Tell students that writers usually get and develop their ideas during the prewriting phase of a writing project. However, writers can still develop or add ideas while they are drafting or revising a piece of writing.

Direct students to the model on page 52 and tell them to imagine that they are revising this personal narrative. Ask *Wouldn't it be good to show how some of the other students enjoyed this experience? And wouldn't it be good to discuss some of the other dishes the students made?*

Point out that these are ideas that could be added during either the drafting or revising phases. Then work with students to list possible details that might develop these ideas, such as:

My friend Alma thought it was the best Thanksgiving she had ever had, too.

We also made turkey, cranberry sauce, and mashed potatoes.

Summary

Minilesson 41	Minilesson 42

Using Your Own Words

Objective: Use your own words to summarize.

Guiding Question: How do I retell a story in my own words?

Teach/Model—I Do

With students, read and discuss Parts of a Story Summary and the model on handbook p. 54. Explain that, in a summary, writers use their own words to tell about the most important events in a story. Point out the part of the model that says *On the day of the test, there is a horrible storm.* Then read the description from the text *It was one of those storms where the rain came down in washtubs, but the stage was scheduled to go.* Point out how the summary gives just the essential information about what happened.

Guided Practice—We Do

Choose a reading selection the whole class has read. Then work together to identify the main events in the text. Write the events on the board. Have volunteers summarize the selection in their own words.

Practice/Apply—You Do

COLLABORATIVE Choose a passage from a story, such as "The World According to Humphrey," and write it on the board: *They talked and talked and Dad got out some cards and they played a game called Crazy Eights and another one called Pig where they put their fingers on their noses and laughed like hyenas.* Have groups work together to summarize the passage.

INDEPENDENT Have students choose another passage from the same story and summarize it in their own words.

Conference/Evaluate

Circulate and help students determine which details are important and which are not needed.

Drafting a Summary

Objective: Write a summary of the main events in a story.

Guiding Question: How can I describe what a story is about in a few sentences?

Teach/Model—I Do

Have students review handbook p. 54. Read the model aloud, pointing out the topic sentence, the story problem, the main events, and the boldfaced transitions. Go over the list in the Other Transitions box.

Guided Practice—We Do

We Do 1 Help students choose a reading selection to summarize. Guide them to name the story problem and the important events. Write phrases they suggest on the board. Then work with students to put those events into sentences to complete the frame. Have students write in their books as you write on the board.

Practice/Apply—You Do

You Do 2 **COLLABORATIVE** Have small groups plan and complete Activity 2. Have them choose a story, list the story's problem and important events, and then fill in the frame. Remind them to use transitions to organize and link ideas. Groups can then share their writing.

You Do 3 **INDEPENDENT** Have students read the directions. Tell them to use their prewriting plan from Lesson 21 or to brainstorm a new plan using Graphic Organizer 4.

Conference/Evaluate

As students draft, circulate and help them determine which details are important and which are not needed in a summary. Evaluate using the rubric on p. 104.

Digital
- eBook
- WriteSmart
- Interactive Lessons

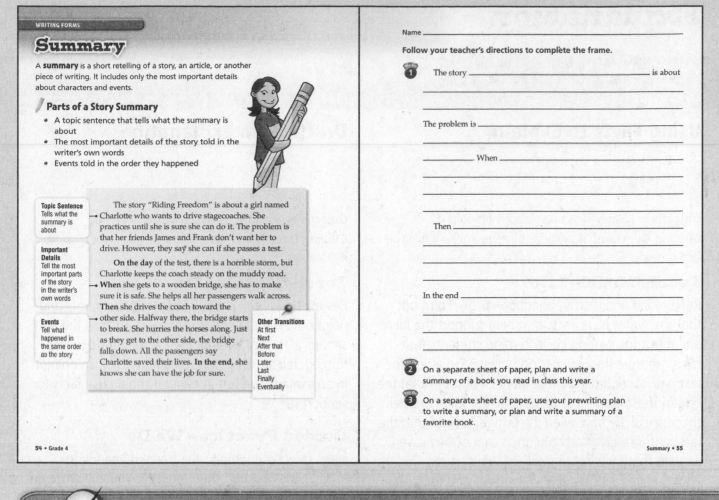

Summary

A **summary** is a short retelling of a story, an article, or another piece of writing. It includes only the most important details about characters and events.

Parts of a Story Summary

- A topic sentence that tells what the summary is about
- The most important details of the story told in the writer's own words
- Events told in the order they happened

Topic Sentence
Tells what the summary is about

Important Details
Tell the most important parts of the story in the writer's own words

Events
Tell what happened in the same order as the story

The story "Riding Freedom" is about a girl named Charlotte who wants to drive stagecoaches. She practices until she is sure she can do it. The problem is that her friends James and Frank don't want her to drive. However, they say she can if she passes a test.

On the day of the test, there is a horrible storm, but Charlotte keeps the coach steady on the muddy road. **When** she gets to a wooden bridge, she has to make sure it is safe. She helps all her passengers walk across. **Then** she drives the coach toward the other side. Halfway there, the bridge starts to break. She hurries the horses along. Just as they get to the other side, the bridge falls down. All the passengers say Charlotte saved their lives. **In the end,** she knows she can have the job for sure.

Other Transitions
At first
Next
After that
Before
Later
Last
Finally
Eventually

54 • Grade 4

Name _____

Follow your teacher's directions to complete the frame.

1 The story _____ is about _____

The problem is _____

_____ When _____

Then _____

In the end _____

2 On a separate sheet of paper, plan and write a summary of a book you read in class this year.

3 On a separate sheet of paper, use your prewriting plan to write a summary, or plan and write a summary of a favorite book.

Summary • 55

Corrective Feedback

IF . . . students have trouble deciding what is important to include in their summary,

THEN . . . have them ask themselves the *five Ws and an H: who? what? when? where? why? how?* Their summary should briefly answer all of these questions.

Focus Trait: Evidence

Remind students that a summary does not have to include every detail from a story. Removing unimportant details will make a summary clearer and easier to understand. Write the following on the board:

The television was broken. Andrew liked to watch shows about gadgets. Andrew and his sister went outside. They played a game with their neighbors.

Ask students to identify which detail in the paragraph is less important than the others. (*Andrew liked to watch shows about gadgets.*) Have students suggest ways to rewrite the paragraph to include only important details.

Grade 4 • 55

Explanation

Minilesson 43

Using Facts to Explain

Objective: Identify facts to explain nonfiction text.

Guiding Question: How do facts help to explain a thing or event?

Teach/Model—I Do

Read aloud and discuss handbook p. 56. Point out that the writer gave facts that help support the ideas and make the writing clear. Remind students that facts are true; they are not opinions. Read aloud the last pair of sentences in the model. Point out that the first of these sentences gives concrete facts that tell readers exactly how wide the bridge is. Note that the last sentence gives an opinion; it cannot be proven. Explain that facts come from reliable sources—books, encyclopedias, and websites—and that writers should verify, or check, facts they use.

Guided Practice—We Do

Work with students to think of facts that might be added to make the model even more interesting *(its height, people who explored the area)*. Then work with students to write, on the board, other explanatory text topics, such as *How was the Lincoln Memorial built?* Work with students to write several facts about the topic you would like to know, such as *Who built it? What material was used?*

Practice/Apply—You Do

COLLABORATIVE Tell groups to use the topic *Bronx Zoo* for generating facts. Have them write a list of details they would need to learn to explain their topic.

INDEPENDENT Have students choose another topic and list facts they would need to find out in order to explain the topic.

Conference/Evaluate

Have students evaluate their lists to make sure they refer to facts they would need to look up.

Minilesson 44

Drafting an Explanation

Objective: Use facts to explain a thing or event.

Guiding Question: How can I use facts to make an explanation clearer?

Teach/Model—I Do

Review handbook p. 56. Read aloud the model and point out how the writer uses facts, such as the first sentence, to explain how the Rainbow Bridge was formed. Tell students that they may voice an opinion in an explanation but in general should use facts to support it.

Guided Practice—We Do

We Do 1 Direct students to the frame on handbook p. 57. Mention that, together, you will write an explanation about how the Washington Monument was built. Model how to look up facts on reputable websites. Then work with students to write an introduction and add facts such as *The Washington Monument reaches more than 555 feet in height.* Together complete the frame. Have students write in their books as you write on the board.

Practice/Apply—You Do

You Do 2 **COLLABORATIVE** Have groups plan and complete Activity 2. Tell them to use websites, books, and encyclopedias to find facts. Have groups share what they have written.

You Do 3 **INDEPENDENT** Have students read and follow the directions. Tell them to use their prewriting plan from Lesson 22 or brainstorm a new plan using Graphic Organizer 3.

Conference/Evaluate

As students draft, have them evaluate their work using the rubric on p. 104.

 Digital
- eBook
- WriteSmart
- Interactive Lessons

Explanation

An **explanation** is writing that explains, or tells why or how something happens. The purpose of an explanation is to give readers information about a topic.

Parts of an Explanation
- A beginning that introduces the topic
- Information that is organized in a way that makes sense
- Facts and examples that support the topic
- An ending that sums up the main points

Beginning
Tells what the explanation is about

Organization
Presents information in a way that makes sense

Facts and Examples
Include details that help develop the explanation

Ending
Draws the explanation to a close

→ Rainbow Bridge in southern Utah was formed millions of years ago. Rain and melted snow ran down Navajo Mountain. **When** the water flowed off the mountain, it created Bridge Creek. As the creek flowed toward the Colorado River, it passed through a canyon.
→ For centuries, the creek washed over layers of rock in the canyon. The rushing water slowly wore away the rock **so that** it created thin rock walls. Eventually, the water broke through the thin walls and made a hole.
→ **As a result**, a colorful stone bridge was carved out of the rock. The bottom of the bridge is reddish brown. The top is pink with dark red streaks. These rich colors come from iron and other minerals. Today, Rainbow Bridge arches high above Bridge Creek. It stretches more than 200 feet from
→ one side to the other. Rainbow Bridge is one of the world's natural wonders!

Other Transitions
Because
Thus
Therefore
Consequently
In order to
Since
Accordingly
For this reason

Name _____

Follow your teacher's directions to complete the frame.

1 _____
_____
_____ because
_____
_____ Since _____
_____
_____ . Therefore, _____
_____
_____ . _____
_____ so that _____
_____
For this reason, _____
_____
_____ . As a result _____
_____
_____

2 On a separate sheet of paper, write an explanation about an important event in the history of your community or state.

3 On a separate sheet of paper, use your prewriting plan to write an explanation, or make a new plan to write about what causes a certain weather event, such as clouds or a rainbow.

✔ Corrective Feedback

IF . . . students are having a hard time coming up with facts,

THEN . . . remind them that a fact is something that can be proven. For example, *The Washington Monument is 555 feet and 5 1/8 inches tall* can be proven because the monument can be measured. Have students write down a few facts and opinions, exchange papers with partners, and discuss which items are facts and which are opinions.

Focus Trait: Elaboration

Tell students that, when they write an explanation, they can make it more interesting by elaborating and using details. Write the following sentences on the board: *The Amazon River is long. It is the second longest river in the world.* Help volunteers connect the sentences to make the details clearer. *(The Amazon River is the second longest river in the world.)* Explain that there are other ways to use elaboration to make sentences clearer, such as breaking up sentences that are too long, beginning sentences in different ways, and varying the lengths of the sentences. Using the model, have students identify specific examples of elaboration that are clear and show the meaning the writer intends. Then have students revise their own explanations to make their sentences clear.

Procedural Composition

Minilesson 45

Using Sequential Order

Objective: Use sequential order for sets of instructions.

Guiding Question: How can I best show the order of steps?

Teach/Model—I Do

Point to the model on handbook p. 58. Tell students that, when they write instructions for a Procedural Composition, they need to plan and organize their ideas in sequential, or time, order. Point out the steps shown in the model, and explain that they are in exactly the same order in which the process should be done. Emphasize this by making a flow chart that shows the steps in order.

Guided Practice—We Do

On the board, write a set of instructions out of order. For example: *Rinse your mouth. Move the toothbrush up and down to clean your teeth. Put toothpaste on your toothbrush.* Draw a flow chart on the board and help students place the steps in sequential order.

Practice/Apply—You Do

COLLABORATIVE On the board, write another set of instructions, such as *Dry your hands on a towel. Turn on warm water. Rub your hands together under the water for at least twenty seconds.* Have groups use flowcharts to organize the steps in sequential order.

INDEPENDENT Write a third set of instructions on the board, such as *Press the two slices of bread together. Spread peanut butter on one slice of bread. Spread jelly on another slice of bread.* Have students work on their own to make a flow chart that puts the steps in sequential order.

Conference/Evaluate

With students, clarify how steps build upon one another as the process is carried out. Use questions, such as *Should you press the two slices of bread together before or after you put peanut butter on one slice?*

Minilesson 46

Drafting a Procedural Composition

Objective: Compose clear and sequential instructions.

Guiding Question: How can I explain how to do something?

Teach/Model—I Do

Discuss the model, pointing out the topic sentence, the steps in the process, and the boldfaced transitions on handbook p. 58. Go over the list in the Other Transitions box. Then suggest a familiar process, such as preparing cereal for breakfast. List the steps involved and number them.

Guided Practice—We Do

 Point out the topic sentence in the frame on handbook p. 59. Ask students to name steps they might take to prepare for an important test. Choose four of those suggestions and help students identify the order in which they should be completed. Together, write sentences to complete the frame. Have students write in their books as you write on the board.

Practice/Apply—You Do

 COLLABORATIVE Have groups plan and complete Activity 2. Have them decide on a simple process to describe and then list the steps involved. Have groups share and discuss their writing.

INDEPENDENT Have students read the directions. Tell them to use their prewriting plan from Lesson 23 or to brainstorm a new plan using Graphic Organizer 4.

Conference/Evaluate

Circulate and help students choose transitions that organize ideas sequentially. Evaluate using the rubric on p. 104.

Digital
• eBook
• WriteSmart
• Interactive Lessons

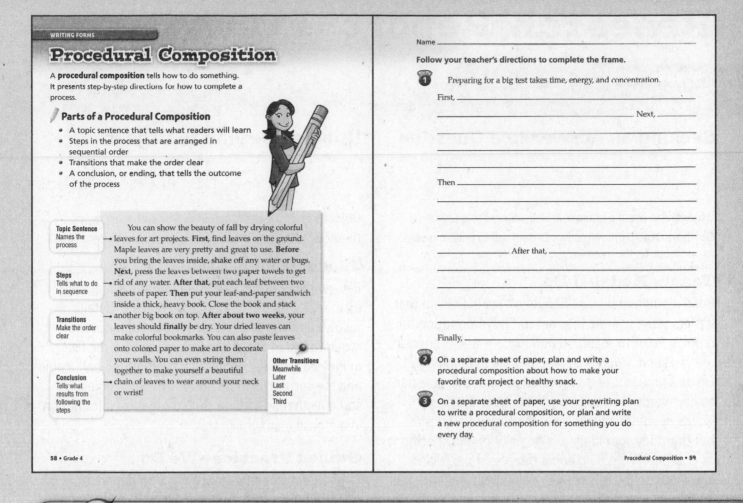

Procedural Composition

A **procedural composition** tells how to do something. It presents step-by-step directions for how to complete a process.

Parts of a Procedural Composition

• A topic sentence that tells what readers will learn
• Steps in the process that are arranged in sequential order
• Transitions that make the order clear
• A conclusion, or ending, that tells the outcome of the process

Topic Sentence
Names the process

Steps
Tells what to do in sequence

Transitions
Make the order clear

Conclusion
Tells what results from following the steps

You can show the beauty of fall by drying colorful leaves for art projects. **First**, find leaves on the ground. Maple leaves are very pretty and great to use. **Before** you bring the leaves inside, shake off any water or bugs. **Next**, press the leaves between two paper towels to get rid of any water. **After that**, put each leaf between two sheets of paper. **Then** put your leaf-and-paper sandwich inside a thick, heavy book. Close the book and stack another big book on top. **After about two weeks**, your leaves should **finally** be dry. Your dried leaves can make colorful bookmarks. You can also paste leaves onto colored paper to make art to decorate your walls. You can even string them together to make yourself a beautiful chain of leaves to wear around your neck or wrist!

Other Transitions
Meanwhile
Later
Last
Second
Third

Name _____

Follow your teacher's directions to complete the frame.

1 Preparing for a big test takes time, energy, and concentration.

First, _____

_____ Next, _____

_____

_____

_____

Then _____

_____

_____

_____ After that, _____

_____

_____

_____

_____

Finally, _____

2 On a separate sheet of paper, plan and write a procedural composition about how to make your favorite craft project or healthy snack.

3 On a separate sheet of paper, use your prewriting plan to write a procedural composition, or plan and write a new procedural composition for something you do every day.

✓ Corrective Feedback

IF . . . students have difficulty including all the necessary steps in their instructions,

THEN . . . have them draw separate, simple cartoons of the steps they can visualize in the process. Have them arrange the cartoons in order and then ask a partner to "narrate" the process. Any missing steps should become obvious.

Focus Trait: Organization

Tell students that they can do two things that can help organize information in sequential order. First, they can write the descriptions of steps in order in their instructions. Then they can use transition words to make the order and connections clear. On the board, write:

Buy soil, seeds, and trays. Fill trays with soil. Plant seeds one inch apart. Water seeds daily. Watch them sprout.

Review the boldfaced transition words in the model and the Other Transitions on handbook p. 58. Then have students suggest transitions to add to the paragraph on the board. Remind them that their transitions should make the paragraph clearer and flow more smoothly. Possible answer:

Before you begin, buy soil, seeds, and trays. First, fill trays with soil. Next, plant seeds one inch apart. Then, water seeds daily. Finally, watch them sprout.

Research Report: Prewriting

Minilesson 47

Seeking an Answer to a Question

Objective: Use the Internet to find answers to questions.

Guiding Question: What words can I use to find an answer to questions on the Internet?

Teach/Model—I Do

Read aloud and discuss handbook p. 60. Explain that writers often use the Internet to find information for reports. Point to section II and explain that it answers the question, *What are some threats to bald eagles?* Discuss how to use a shortened form of this question as key words for a search engine. Note that key words need not always be in the form of a question but that they should always be as brief and specific as possible. Write *bald eagle threats* on the board and discuss why this phrase would be useful for finding information.

Guided Practice—We Do

On the board, write a research question, such as *How far away is the moon from Earth?* Write student suggestions for key words for an Internet search for the answers to this question. Work with students to practice leaving out unimportant words and emphasizing important ones (for example, *distance Earth moon*).

Practice/Apply—You Do

COLLABORATIVE Write several other research questions, such as *What are the different kinds of squirrels?* or *What important things did President Abraham Lincoln do?* Have groups choose one question and write key words for an Internet search.

INDEPENDENT Have students choose another question and write key words on their own.

Conference/Evaluate

Have students evaluate their key words to determine if they will answer the question.

Minilesson 48

Using an Outline to Organize

Objective: Make an organized outline with main topics.

Guiding Question: What main topics belong in my outline?

Teach/Model—I Do

Review handbook p. 60. Explain that in an outline, main topics follow Roman numerals and details follow capital or lower-case letters. Point out the organization of the outline, showing how the first main idea includes general facts about the bald eagle and the second includes threats to bald eagles. Tell students that an outline should organize information in a logical manner like this.

Guided Practice—We Do

 Direct students to Activity 1 on handbook p. 61. Tell them that, together, you will write an outline about grizzly bears. Work with students to find information on the Internet. On the board, write main ideas such as *physical description*. Help students discuss which main ideas and details to include as well as ways to organize the outline. Guide them to complete the frame. Have students write in their books as you write on the board.

Practice/Apply—You Do

 COLLABORATIVE Have groups plan and complete Activity 2. Have groups share what they have written.

INDEPENDENT Have students read and follow the directions. Tell them to use their prewriting plan from Lesson 24 or brainstorm a new plan using an outline.

Conference/Evaluate

As students draft, have them evaluate their work using the rubric on p. 104.

> **Digital**
> • eBook
> • WriteSmart
> • Interactive Lessons

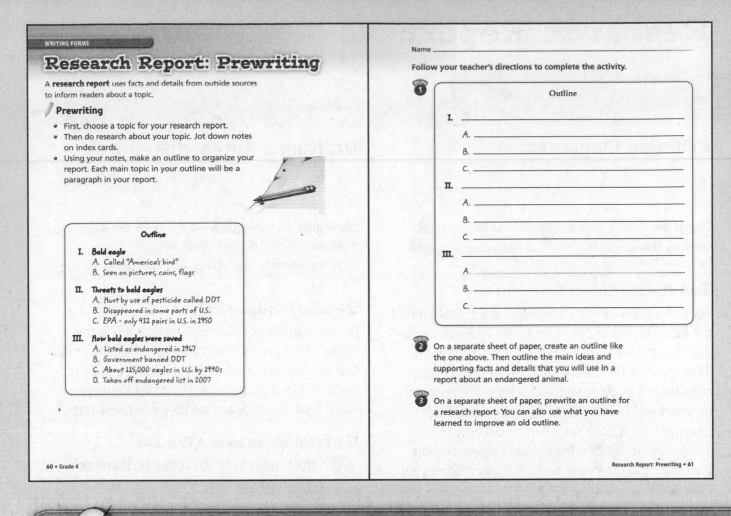

Research Report: Prewriting

A **research report** uses facts and details from outside sources to inform readers about a topic.

Prewriting

- First, choose a topic for your research report.
- Then do research about your topic. Jot down notes on index cards.
- Using your notes, make an outline to organize your report. Each main topic in your outline will be a paragraph in your report.

Outline

I. **Bald eagle**
   A. Called "America's bird"
   B. Seen on pictures, coins, flags

II. **Threats to bald eagles**
   A. Hurt by use of pesticide called DDT
   B. Disappeared in some parts of U.S.
   C. EPA - only 412 pairs in U.S. in 1950

III. **How bald eagles were saved**
   A. Listed as endangered in 1967
   B. Government banned DDT
   C. About 115,000 eagles in U.S. by 1990s
   D. Taken off endangered list in 2007

Name _____

Follow your teacher's directions to complete the activity.

1

Outline

I. _____
   A. _____
   B. _____
   C. _____

II. _____
   A. _____
   B. _____
   C. _____

III. _____
   A. _____
   B. _____
   C. _____

2 On a separate sheet of paper, create an outline like the one above. Then outline the main ideas and supporting facts and details that you will use in a report about an endangered animal.

3 On a separate sheet of paper, prewrite an outline for a research report. You can also use what you have learned to improve an old outline.

✓ Corrective Feedback

IF . . . students are having a hard time coming up with key words for research,

THEN . . . have them work with the indexes of various informational texts. Explain that the terms found in an index often include key words that can help readers find information on the Internet. For example, in a book about the cardinal, possible index terms might be *habitat* or *life cycle*. Have students choose a few key words from an index and then study the page or pages on which they find information about those key words. Then have them practice using these key words for an Internet search.

Focus Trait: Organization

Tell students that outlining is a good way to organize ideas. However, some students may find that once they begin outlining, their topics are too broad and their outline is too long. Explain that when this happens, writers can narrow their topic focus by asking questions such as *What kind?* For example, if a student's topic is *Owls*, one way to narrow the topic is to focus on one kind of owl, such as the barn owl.

Model narrowing the number of ideas in a report by narrowing the topic. Write *Flags* on the board and ask students to name kinds of flags, such as their state flag or the American flag. Point out that now that the topic has been narrowed, it is easier to research and write about it. Write several other broad topics on the board, such as *Flowers*, *State Symbols*, and *Dogs*, and have students come up with narrower topics by asking *What kind?*

Grade 4 • **61**

Research Report

Minilesson 49

Avoiding Plagiarism

Objective: Write in your own words to avoid plagiarism.

Guiding Question: How can I use information from other sources and rewrite it in my own words?

Teach/Model—I Do

Read aloud and discuss handbook p. 62. Explain that the facts the writer used came from research sources and that the writer paraphrased them, or rewrote them in his or her own words. Tell students that *plagiarism* is copying someone else's writing word for word and that it should never be done. Find a passage from a book and then model how to paraphrase it, reading the passage aloud, closing the book, and then rewriting what you read in your own words.

Guided Practice—We Do

Write a sentence on the board from a book or website, such as *Visitors look in wonder at the one-mile deep, 277-mile long Grand Canyon.* Read the passage aloud several times and then erase it. Work with students to rewrite the sentence in their own words. For example: *The Grand Canyon is one mile deep and 277 miles long. It is a thrilling sight.*

Practice/Apply—You Do

COLLABORATIVE Have students find a passage from an informational text and read it several times. As they read, tell them to note key ideas and details and paraphrase them. Then have students close the book and rewrite the passage in their own words

INDEPENDENT Have students choose another passage and rewrite it in their own words.

Conference/Evaluate

Have students compare their rewrites with the original sources to make sure they didn't plagiarize.

Minilesson 50

Drafting a Research Report

Objective: Draft a research report with an introduction, facts to support main ideas, and a conclusion.

Guiding Question: What ideas do I want to include in my draft?

Teach/Model—I Do

Review handbook p. 62. Explain that this is the writer's final version; before writing this, the writer first did research and wrote an outline and then wrote a first draft. Point out that first drafts help writers get down ideas that they can revise later.

Guided Practice—We Do

We Do 1 Direct students to the frame on handbook p. 63. With students review the research and outline you did together in Minilesson 48. Work with them to write a first draft based on the notes and outline. Write suggestions for one of the main ideas on the board, such as *description: Grizzly bears can weigh up to 790 pounds or more.* Together, complete the frame. Have students write in their books as you write on the board.

Practice/Apply—You Do

You Do 2 **COLLABORATIVE** Have groups complete Activity 2. Remind them that they will revise and proofread later. Have groups share their work.

You Do 3 **INDEPENDENT** Have students read and follow the directions. Tell them to use their prewriting plan from Lesson 25 or brainstorm a new plan using an outline.

Conference/Evaluate

As students draft, have them evaluate their work using the rubric or on p. 104.

Digital
- eBook
- WriteSmart
- Interactive Lessons

Research Report

A **research report** gives information about a topic. It uses outside sources for facts and details.

Parts of a Research Report

- An introduction to the report
- Facts and details that support a main idea
- Information from different sources, such as books, magazines, and the Internet
- The names of the sources that provided information
- A conclusion that sums up the main points

Introduction Tells what the report will be about	The bald eagle has been called "America's bird." This beautiful animal is seen on pictures, coins, and flags. However, not long ago real-life bald eagles almost disappeared from the United States. It took many years of hard work to save them.
Main Idea	The United States Department of the Interior says that for years bald eagles and their eggs were hurt by DDT, a pesticide. Before long, the birds had almost disappeared in some parts of the country. Finally, **in 1967**, the government listed eagles as endangered. This protected the birds from hunters and other enemies. **Then** the government banned DDT.
Facts Support the main idea	
Information Source Tells where paraphrased information was found	These steps helped the birds come back. According to the Environmental Protection Agency, there were 412 pairs of bald eagles in the United States in 1950. By the 1990s, though, there were almost 115,000 eagles in this country.
Conclusion Sums up the main idea	**Because** the bald eagle has done so well, it was taken off the endangered list in 2007. Today, its future is looking good.

Other Transitions
First
After
In addition
Since
As a result
In the end
According to

Name _____

Follow your teacher's directions to complete the frame.

1 (Introduction) _____

(Main idea, factual details) _____

(Main idea, factual details) _____

In conclusion, _____

2 On a separate sheet of paper, write a research report about an endangered animal.

3 On a separate sheet of paper, use your prewriting plan to write a research report, or plan and write a report about a new technology.

✔ Corrective Feedback

IF . . . students are having a hard time rewriting information in their own words,

THEN . . . have them use a thesaurus to find synonyms for words in the original passage. Explain that they can find synonyms for words in the original text and use these words when they paraphrase. Emphasize that it takes more than simply replacing words with synonyms to avoid plagiarism, however; have them practice using different sentence structures or even breaking up a long sentence or combining several short ones.

Focus Trait: Elaboration

Tell students that when they write a research report, it is important to elaborate on your ideas by using descriptive words that create a mental picture for the reader. Nouns and adjectives should be specific, not general, and there should be strong, specific action verbs as well. On the board, write *Grizzlies have blond to black fur with white or gray ends.* Ask students to point to "dull" or "overly general" words. Then ask students to offer suggestions for improving them. For example, the opening words could be replaced with the more vivid words. Likewise, the rest of the sentence can be made both more vivid and more precise (for example: *Grizzlies range in color from golden blond to dark black, with fur that usually glistens with white or gray tips.*)

Response to Fiction

Minilesson 51

Using Examples from the Text

Objective: Use examples from a text to support a response.

Guiding Question: How can I support my opinion about a text with examples?

Teach/Model—I Do

With students, read and then discuss handbook p. 64. Point out that the model gives the writer's opinion about a story character and supports it with examples from the story. Read the first paragraph, explaining that it states the reader's opinion that Stormy is a great character. Point out reasons and examples that support the opinion (reasons: *he's a great adventurer*; *he's courageous*; examples: *he goes to sea, farms, sees the world*; *he battles an octopus*). Explain that words such as *for instance* and *in addition* help link the opinion and reasons.

Guided Practice—We Do

Help students choose a story they all have read and guide them to give opinions about a character in it. Then help students identify examples that support their opinions.

Practice/Apply—You Do

COLLABORATIVE Guide students to look back at another story they read together. Have small groups write a sentence stating their opinion of a character. Then ask groups to write at least one example from the story that supports the opinion.

INDEPENDENT Have students write a sentence stating their opinion of another character from the same story. Have them find one or two examples in the story to support their opinion.

Conference/Evaluate

Encourage students having trouble writing an opinion to use judgment words, such as *think, feel, believe, best*, or *worst*. Point out that these words are used to state opinions and personal feelings about a topic.

Minilesson 52

Drafting a Response to Fiction

Objective: Write a response to fiction.

Guiding Question: How can I best support my opinion?

Teach/Model—I Do

Review handbook p. 64. Point out the writer's opinion in the model and the reasons and examples that support it. Remind students that the boldfaced transitions in the model link the writer's opinion to reasons. Point out the descriptive words in the Character Words box.

Guided Practice—We Do

We Do 1 Direct students to the frame on handbook p. 65. Help students complete the topic sentence, using a character from another story they have read. Work with students to identify reasons why the character is interesting. Have them suggest sentences to complete the frame giving examples that support their opinions. Have students write in their books as you write on the board.

Practice/Apply—You Do

You Do 2 **COLLABORATIVE** Have small groups plan and complete Activity 2. Tell them to complete the topic sentence with their group's opinion and then finish the paragraph together. Have groups share and discuss their work.

You Do 3 **INDEPENDENT** Have students read the directions. Ask them to use their prewriting plan from Lesson 26 or use Graphic Organizer 7 to brainstorm a new plan.

Conference/Evaluate

As students draft, circulate and help them choose examples that support their opinions. Evaluate using the rubric on p. 104.

 Digital
- eBook
- WriteSmart
- Interactive Lessons

Response to Fiction

A **response to fiction** is a composition that explains a writer's thoughts and feelings about a piece of literature. The response can be about a novel, story, or play.

Parts of a Response to Fiction

- An introduction that states the writer's opinion
- Reasons that explain the writer's opinion
- Examples from the text that support the reasons
- A conclusion that sums up the ideas

Introduction States the writer's opinion	"Stormalong," by Mary Pope Osborne, tells the story of a great character. Alfred Bulltop Stormalong, called Stormy, is a giant. He is giant in size but in other ways, too.
Supporting Sentences Give reasons for the opinion	**First,** Stormy's actions are bigger than life. He is a great adventurer. He goes to sea, grows millions of potatoes in Kansas, and then goes back to sea and travels all over the world.
Examples Support the reasons	**In addition,** Stormy's courage is as large as his size. For example, he battles a huge octopus and survives terrible storms.
Conclusion Sums up the ideas	Stormy is a giant who is adventurous and courageous. **Because of this,** I think he is a character that anyone would enjoy reading about.

Character Words
thoughtful
shy
gentle
honest
loyal
humorous
wise
clever

Name _____

Follow your teacher's directions to complete the frame.

1 One of the most interesting characters I've ever read about in a story is
_____
_____

For instance, _____
_____
_____
_____
_____

_____ In addition, _____
_____
_____
_____
_____

Because of this, _____
_____
_____
_____

2 On a separate sheet of paper, plan and write a response to your favorite fairy tale.

3 On a separate sheet of paper, use your prewriting plan to write a response to fiction, or plan and write a new response about a book, story, or character you really enjoyed.

Corrective Feedback

IF . . . students are unable to come up with at least one example to support their opinion,

THEN . . . have them ask themselves, *Why do I like/dislike this book/story/character?* The answer to the question should lead them to an example in the work that supports their opinion.

Focus Trait: Elaboration

Remind students that using specific words will help readers understand their opinions about a piece of fiction. It will also help readers understand their opinions about a piece of fiction. Write this statement on the board:

I *like* Maniac Magee *because the main character is great.* Elicit from students how the opinion can be strengthened by using a more specific word.

Example: *I liked Maniac Magee because the main character is unique and gets into all sorts of trouble.*

Have partners revise the words they can make more specific.

Journal Entry

Expressing Thoughts and Feelings

Objective: Express thoughts and feelings in writing.

Guiding Question: How can I get my readers to understand what I thought and how I felt?

Teach/Model—I Do

Read aloud and discuss handbook p. 66. Explain that, in a journal entry, writers include personal thoughts and feelings about an event. These help readers understand what happened and how the event affected the writer. Point to examples of what the model writer thought and felt about the experience. (Example: *I was a little bit nervous because…*) Discuss how these sentences help readers better understand the writer and the event.

Guided Practice—We Do

On the board, write a few scenes that will evoke feelings in children, such as *taking a big test* or *winning a game or contest.* Tell students to place themselves in one of these scenes. Help them come up with words that describe their feelings, such as *My heart pounded.* Write their descriptions on the board.

Practice/Apply—You Do

COLLABORATIVE Have small groups choose an event you listed or another event they have experienced. Have them work together to create a few sentences they might include in a journal entry about it. Tell them to include their thoughts and feelings about the event.

INDEPENDENT Have students choose an event on their own and express their thoughts and feelings about it.

Conference/Evaluate

Encourage students to ask themselves, *Did I use words and phrases that help readers understand how I felt and what I thought?*

Drafting a Journal Entry

Objective: Write a journal entry that is clear and thoughtful.

Guiding Question: How can I clearly describe the event and let readers understand how it made me feel?

Teach/Model—I Do

Review handbook p. 66, noting how the writer uses details and sequence words to help readers imagine the setting and follow the action. Explain that the writer also uses words that relate to the senses and feelings to bring the events to life.

Guided Practice—We Do

We Do 1 Direct students to the frame on handbook p. 67. Tell them that, together, you will write a journal entry about the first day of school. Work with students to "set the scene" in the first paragraph (*It was the first day of school.*). Use sensory details to show what was happening and what feelings came about. Plan and write the sequence of events together, ending with a description of how the writer felt about the event. Have students write in their books as you write on the board.

Practice/Apply—You Do

You Do 2 **COLLABORATIVE** Have groups plan and complete Activity 2. Tell them to set the scene clearly and to use words that express their thoughts and feelings. Have groups share what they have written.

You Do 3 **INDEPENDENT** Have students read and follow the directions. Tell them to use their prewriting plan from Lesson 27 or brainstorm a new plan using Graphic Organizer 10.

Conference/Evaluate

As students draft, have them evaluate their work using the rubric on p. 104.

Digital
- eBook
- WriteSmart
- Interactive Lessons

Journal Entry

A **journal entry** is an item written in a journal or diary. A journal entry explores the writer's experiences, thoughts, and feelings. It can include daily observations, facts, and important personal experiences.

Parts of a Journal Entry

- A beginning that introduces the topic
- Facts about what happened, when it happened, who was involved, and where they were
- Vivid details that come from the five senses
- An ending that tells what the writer learned or how the event ended

Beginning
Tells what the entry is about

Facts
Tell who, what, where, when, why

Sensory Details
Include sights, sounds, smells, tastes, and feelings

Ending
Tells how the event ended and how the writer felt

August 14, 2012

Today I went to my grandmother's house and she taught me how to bake bread. I was a little bit nervous because she is a great cook and I'd never made bread before. I asked Nona to share her bread recipe because someday I might want to pass it on to my own children.

First, Nona let me mix the ingredients, which included flour, yeast, milk, oil, water, and salt. She showed me how to knead the dough by squeezing and mashing it. **Then** we put the bowl of dough on a windowsill where it rose and doubled in size. **Next**, I shaped the dough and put it in bread pans. In the oven, the dough turned golden brown. When the bread was done, we ate warm slices with melted butter. Yum! Nona said that I did a good job. I feel proud that now I can make bread like Nona does.

Other Transitions
Because
After
During
Now
Before
Later
Last
Soon
Earlier

Name _____

Follow your teacher's directions to complete the frame.

1

_____

_____

_____

_____

At first _____

_____

_____ Then _____

_____ Next, _____

Finally, _____

_____

_____ I felt _____

_____

_____

2 On a separate sheet of paper, write a journal entry about a time you were surprised.

3 On a separate sheet of paper, use your prewriting plan to write a journal entry, or make a new plan to write about a holiday you will never forget.

✔ Corrective Feedback

IF . . . students are having a hard time expressing their thoughts and feelings,

THEN . . . have them imagine they are telling a trusted friend about the experience and that this person asks them questions about how they felt or thought about the events. For example, *What exactly were you thinking when you met your new teacher? How were you feeling?* Encourage students to use sensory words to help readers understand their thoughts and feelings. For example, *My palms were sweaty and my heart was racing as I opened the classroom door.*

Focus Trait: Elaboration

Tell students that they can elaborate to make their journals more interesting by using precise words and clear details.

Model elaborating by writing sentences on the board and modifying them so that the writer's personality shows through:

I was scared when the nurse held up the needle.

When the nurse held up the needle, I swallowed hard. It seemed like it was a foot long! My arm

would never be the same!

Work with students to compare the two passages, pointing to words and phrases that let the writer's personality show through.

Write the following sentence on the board. Then work with students to elaborate by rewriting or adding to it: *I was so happy when we won the game.*

Public Service Announcement

Using Language to Affect Audience

Drafting a Public Service Announcement

Objective: Use language that appeals to feelings.

Guiding Question: How can I make my writing more persuasive by using language that targets emotions?

Teach/Model—I Do

Read aloud and discuss handbook p. 68. Explain that a public service announcement uses words that stir up readers' feelings and cause readers to act a certain way. Point out the "Be smart!" in the first paragraph. Explain that this sentence is persuasive because it makes readers feel a certain way: if they don't agree with the writer and take action, they aren't "smart." On the board, write *Keep your friends safe!* Discuss how this sentence appeals to readers' emotions and stirs them to action.

Guided Practice—We Do

On the board, write an idea for a public service announcement, such as *Don't litter!* Work with students to write a sentence that appeals to readers' emotions and persuades them to take action. You may want to give students a frame such as *When you litter, _____.*

Practice/Apply—You Do

COLLABORATIVE Write several other ideas for public service announcements, such as *recycle to reduce waste* and *buckle your seat belts.* Have groups choose one idea and write several sentences that appeal to readers' emotions and stir them to take action.

INDEPENDENT Have students choose another idea and write a few sentences about it on their own.

Conference/Evaluate

Have students evaluate their sentences to make sure they stir readers to action.

Objective: Write a persuasive public service announcement.

Guiding Question: How can I write and organize my public service announcement so that it persuades readers?

Teach/Model—I Do

Review handbook p. 68. Point out the first and last paragraphs, discussing how the writer uses words that appeal to readers' emotions. Discuss the organization, noting how the writer explains the subject, then gives facts to support the subject, and finally ends with a call to action.

Guided Practice—We Do

 Direct students to handbook p. 69. Say that, together, you will write a public service announcement about crossing the street safely. On the board write, *60,000 pedestrians were killed by cars in 2009.* Work with students to use this sentence to write an introduction. Then fill in the frame with supporting details and steps readers can take to safely cross the street. End with a call to action. Have students write in their books as you write on the board.

Practice/Apply—You Do

 COLLABORATIVE Have groups plan and complete Activity 2. Have groups share what they have written.

INDEPENDENT Have students read and follow the directions. Tell them to use their prewriting plan from Lesson 28 or brainstorm a new plan using Graphic Organizer 7.

Conference/Evaluate

As students draft, have them evaluate their work using the rubric on p. 104.

Digital
- eBook
- WriteSmart
- Interactive Lessons

Public Service Announcement

A **public service announcement** is an advertisement that gives helpful information to the community. Public service announcements appear on radio and television and in newspapers and magazines.

Parts of a Public Service Announcement

- An introduction that grabs the audience's attention
- Facts that give helpful information about the topic
- A call to action that urges the audience to do something
- A conclusion that persuades the audience to feel and act a certain way

Introduction
Gets the reader to pay attention

→ School is back in session in Green Valley. Be smart! Pay attention to school bus safety.

Facts
Tell about the topic

→ Did you know that, in this country, about 17,000 students are injured every year just riding the bus to school? They are treated for cuts, sprains, and bruises.

What can you do to have a safe ride? Here are some simple steps:

- **First**, use the handrail while you get on the bus.
- Buckle your seat belt **as soon as** you sit.

Call to Action
Includes specific things for the audience to do

- **During** the trip, talk quietly. Don't distract the driver.
- Only stand up **after** the bus has completely stopped.

Other Transitions
Before
Next
Until
Immediately
As soon as
Meanwhile
Later
Last

Conclusion
Persuades the audience to take part

→ Green Valley students deserve a safe ride to school. Be sure to follow these safety rules every time you ride the bus.

Name _____

Follow your teacher's directions to complete the frame.

1 _____

- First, _____
- Then _____
- Next, _____
- Finally, _____

2 On a separate sheet of paper, write a public service announcement to persuade people in your community to help clean up a local park.

3 On a separate sheet of paper, use your prewriting plan to write a public service announcement, or make a new plan for an announcement persuading classmates to make your school better in some way.

Corrective Feedback

IF . . . students are having difficulty coming up with persuasive words that appeal to readers' emotions,

THEN . . . explain that advertisements often use similar ways to stir up readers' emotions by appealing to such basic needs as safety, health, and love. For example, a public service announcement about exercising every day might include *Stay healthy and live longer by exercising every day.* Point out that this appeals to readers' need to be healthy. Have students think of ways they can stir up their readers' feelings about another basic need.

Focus Trait: Organization

Tell students that they can use a computer to get a sense of how to organize their public service announcements. One way to do this is to read other public service announcements. Students can find public service announcements of a charity, such as the American Red Cross, by doing an Internet search of key words, such as *public service announcement Red Cross.* Explain that they can also find public service announcements posted in various places in their community, such as grocery stores and recreation centers.

Have students read one such announcement and discuss its various parts: (1) an introduction that grabs readers' attention, (2) details that support the opinion presented, (3) and a call to action at the end. Discuss how this organization helps to make the announcement more effective. Have students also identify words and phrases in the announcement that appeal to readers' emotions. Work with students to make an outline showing the organization of the announcement.

Opinion Essay: Prewriting

Minilesson 57

Determining Audience and Purpose

Objective: Identify the purpose and audience for writing.

Guiding Question: How can I determine who my writing is intended for and why I am writing it?

Teach/Model—I Do

Read aloud and discuss handbook p. 70. Explain that the title tells the writer's *purpose*, or reason for writing: to persuade the audience what the best invention was. The purpose of opinion essays is to persuade readers to agree with an opinion you feel strongly about. Before you prewrite, you must decide on a purpose and the audience—or the people you are writing for—because it affects how and what you write: an opinion paper about not littering, for example, might be different for an audience of children as opposed to adults. The audience in the model is *classmates and teacher* because it is a classroom assignment.

Guided Practice—We Do

On the board, write an opinion, such as *Dogs make better pets than cats.* Work with students to identify the purpose. The audience should be people who would be interested in your opinion. Ask students to identify audiences, such as classmates or cat owners, and to explain how they might change what and how they write for each.

Practice/Apply—You Do

COLLABORATIVE Write several other opinions for opinion essays, such as *our classroom needs a pet.* Have groups choose one opinion and write a purpose and audience.

INDEPENDENT Have students choose another opinion and write a purpose and audience.

Conference/Evaluate

Have students evaluate their purpose and audience to make sure they fit together.

Minilesson 58

Supporting an Opinion with Reasons

Objective: Support an opinion with reasons, facts, and details.

Guiding Question: How can I support my opinions?

Teach/Model—I Do

Review handbook p. 70. Point out that in the idea-support map, the writer gives reasons and facts and details to support them. Explain that the writer supports the second reason by writing *Surf Internet*. She also gives other details for each reason. Tell students that, in an opinion essay, giving more than one fact or detail to support a reason makes the writing more persuasive.

Guided Practice—We Do

 Direct students to Activity 1 on handbook p. 71. Tell students that together you will complete an idea-support map on how planting a school garden could be educational, or teach them things. Work with students to decide on the purpose and audience for the essay. Then, together, complete the map with reasons, facts, and details. Have students write in their books as you write on the board.

Practice/Apply—You Do

 COLLABORATIVE Have groups plan and complete Activity 2. Have them share what they have written.

INDEPENDENT Have students read and follow the directions. Tell them to use their prewriting plan from Lesson 29 or brainstorm a new plan using Graphic Organizer 7.

Conference/Evaluate

As students draft, have them evaluate their work using the rubric on p. 104.

Digital
- eBook
- WriteSmart
- Interactive Lessons

Opinion Essay: Prewriting

An **opinion essay** gives the writer's beliefs about a topic. It uses facts and details to explain the writer's opinions.

Prewriting for Opinion Essay

- Brainstorm a list of topics that are important to you. Choose one that you have a strong opinion about.
- Jot down reasons that support your opinion. Think about facts and details that will explain each reason.
- Now use a graphic organizer to plan your opinion essay.

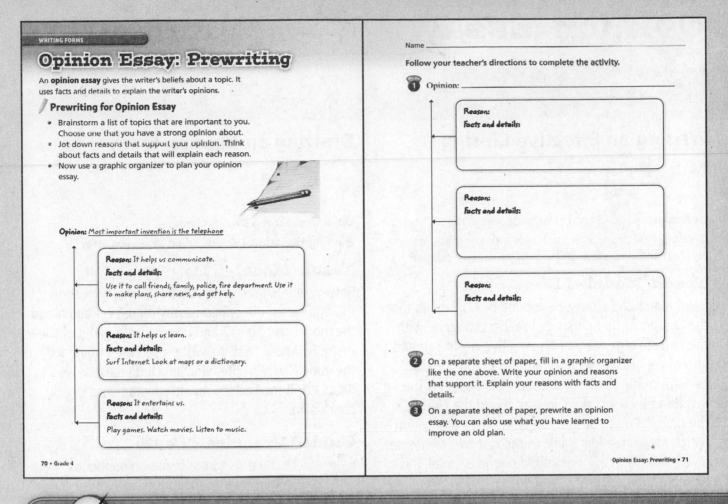

Opinion: Most important invention is the telephone

> **Reason:** It helps us communicate.
> **Facts and details:**
> Use it to call friends, family, police, fire department. Use it to make plans, share news, and get help.

> **Reason:** It helps us learn.
> **Facts and details:**
> Surf Internet. Look at maps or a dictionary.

> **Reason:** It entertains us.
> **Facts and details:**
> Play games. Watch movies. Listen to music.

Name _____

Follow your teacher's directions to complete the activity.

1 Opinion: _____

> **Reason:**
> **Facts and details:**

> **Reason:**
> **Facts and details:**

> **Reason:**
> **Facts and details:**

2 On a separate sheet of paper, fill in a graphic organizer like the one above. Write your opinion and reasons that support it. Explain your reasons with facts and details.

3 On a separate sheet of paper, prewrite an opinion essay. You can also use what you have learned to improve an old plan.

✔ Corrective Feedback

IF . . . students are having a hard time coming up with a purpose and audience,

THEN . . . have them think about something they feel strongly about, such as adopting a classroom pet. Have them ask themselves, *What is something that I care about? What things would I like to see change? What is something that I think is the best or worst, like a movie or book?* Once students have decided on a purpose, have them determine an audience by asking themselves *Who would be interested in reading my opinion? My classmates? My neighbors? My relatives?*

Focus Trait: Purpose

Tell students that when their purpose for writing is to write an opinion essay, they can get ideas for their own essays by reading other opinion essays. Explain that one kind of an opinion essay is an editorial, which often appears in newspapers in the Opinion/Editorial section. Students can go to a newspaper's website and check this section to think about the writer's purpose and the audience the writer is writing for. They can also study the reasons and facts used to support the opinion to think about how to support their own reasons.

Model finding an editorial on a website for a newspaper geared towards children, or print out an editorial to share with students. Have students read the editorial and decide what the purpose for writing is and what details the writer includes to support her opinion. Discuss who they think the writer's audience is and why.

Opinion Essay

Minilesson 59	Minilesson 60

Writing an Effective Closing

Objective: Write a strong, clear, persuasive closing.

Guiding Question: How can I write a closing that sums up my ideas and persuades readers to agree with my opinion?

Teach/Model—I Do

Read aloud and discuss handbook p. 72. Explain that the closing further persuades readers to agree with the writer. Point out that an effective closing should also leave readers with something to think about, perhaps adding new information, because it is the last thing they will read. Reread aloud the closing in the model. Point out that the writer asks a question, which makes readers think. In the last two sentences, he explains that even though a phone is small, it is extremely important.

Guided Practice—We Do

On the board, write *The phone is the most important invention.* Work with students to think of another closing that sums up the opinion and/or leaves the audience with something to think about. Print out a short article about the phone today and have students use facts from it. For example, *There are almost 300 million cell phones in our country today. That's almost one phone for every American!*

Practice/Apply—You Do

COLLABORATIVE Have groups come up with other closings for the telephone essay, either using the facts you provided or restating the opinion in other ways. Remind students to leave readers with something to think about.

INDEPENDENT Have students write another closing on their own.

Conference/Evaluate

Have students evaluate their closing to make sure it restates the opinion and is memorable.

Drafting an Opinion Essay

Objective: Write a strong opinion essay.

Guiding Question: How do I draft an opinion essay?

Teach/Model—I Do

Review with students handbook p. 70, which shows the outline for the opinion essay on p. 72. Read aloud the model on page 72 and point out the parts of the essay. Point out that the writer used the outline for the middle paragraphs, which include reasons and details, and then added an introduction and conclusion.

Guided Practice—We Do

We Do 1 Direct students to the frame on handbook p. 73. Then refer to the graphic organizer they filled out on p. 71 about why planting a garden is educational. Tell students that together you will draft an opinion essay about this topic. Work with students to study the outline and decide what to put in the frame. Then, together, complete the frame, adding a beginning and an ending. Help students suggest strong endings. Have students write in their books as you write on the board.

Practice/Apply—You Do

You Do 2 **COLLABORATIVE** Have groups plan and complete Activity 2. Tell them to write a strong ending. Have groups share what they have written.

You Do 3 **INDEPENDENT** Have students read and follow the directions. Tell them to use their prewriting plan from Lesson 30 or brainstorm a new plan using Graphic Organizer 7.

Conference/Evaluate

As students draft, have them evaluate their work using the rubric on p. 104.

 Digital
- eBook
- WriteSmart
- Interactive Lessons

Opinion Essay

An **opinion essay** expresses the writer's beliefs about a topic. An opinion is a statement that cannot be proved true.

Parts of an Opinion Essay

- A beginning that introduces the topic and states the writer's opinion
- Strong reasons that support the writer's opinion
- Facts and details that explain each reason
- Reasons that are organized in a logical order
- An ending that sums up the writer's opinion

Beginning Identifies the topic and the writer's opinion →

Alexander Graham Bell invented the telephone in 1876. In my opinion, the telephone is the most important invention ever.

Body Paragraphs List reasons in order of importance

One reason is that the telephone helps us communicate. **For example**, we use it to call our family and friends. We use it to make plans or share news. We use it to call the police or fire department if we need help.

Facts and Details Explain the reasons for the writer's opinion

Another reason is that the telephone helps us learn. We use it to get information from the Internet. Or we use it to look at maps or a dictionary.

Ending Tells why your opinion makes sense

Finally, telephones entertain us. We use them to play games. We can watch movies on them. We can **also** use them to listen to music.

Can you imagine life without a phone? This invention fits in a pocket. But it connects us to the whole world.

Other Transitions
For instance
In order to
Most importantly
Mainly
In addition
Most significant
Least important
In fact

Name _____

Follow your teacher's directions to complete the frame.

1 I believe that _____

_____

_____

One reason is that _____

_____

_____

Second, _____

_____

_____

Finally, _____

_____

_____

_____ . For example, _____

_____

In conclusion, _____

_____

2 On a separate sheet of paper, write an opinion essay about another invention that you think is important. Be sure to support your opinion with strong reasons.

3 On a separate sheet of paper, use your prewriting plan to write an opinion essay, or make a new plan to write about a custom or tradition you feel strongly about.

Corrective Evidence

IF . . . students are having a hard time coming up with an effective closing,

THEN . . . have them reread the model and decide how the writer's conclusion makes them think about what life would be like without the telephone. Tell them to ask themselves questions such as, *How would my life be different without _____? How can I expand on this idea to create an effective closing?* In addition, have them reread the information you printed out to find facts they might include in the closing to leave the reader with something to think about.

Focus Trait: Elaboration

Tell students that writers of opinion essays try to hold readers' attention by making their reasons and evidence interesting as well as convincing. Point out that one way to make writing sound more interesting is to replace everyday words and phrases with language that is more descriptive and precise. On the board, write *The telephone is used for a lot of things. The telephone lets us talk to people.* Guide students to suggest ways to replace common,

everyday words and phrases such as "a lot of things" and "lets us talk to people" with more descriptive or precise language. For example, *The telephone is used for a wide variety of purposes. The telephone allows us to communicate with anyone at a moment's notice.* Discuss with students why these sentences are more interesting to read than the previous ones.

Prewriting

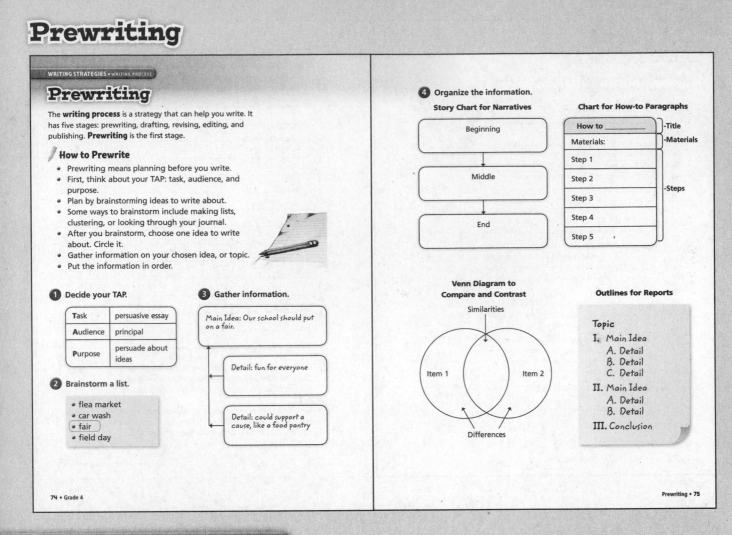

Prewriting

The **writing process** is a strategy that can help you write. It has five stages: prewriting, drafting, revising, editing, and publishing. **Prewriting** is the first stage.

How to Prewrite
- Prewriting means planning before you write.
- First, think about your TAP: task, audience, and purpose.
- Plan by brainstorming ideas to write about.
- Some ways to brainstorm include making lists, clustering, or looking through your journal.
- After you brainstorm, choose one idea to write about. Circle it.
- Gather information on your chosen idea, or topic.
- Put the information in order.

1 Decide your TAP.

Task	persuasive essay
Audience	principal
Purpose	persuade about ideas

2 Brainstorm a list.
- flea market
- car wash
- fair
- field day

3 Gather information.

Main Idea: Our school should put on a fair.

Detail: fun for everyone

Detail: could support a cause, like a food pantry

4 Organize the information.

Story Chart for Narratives

Beginning → Middle → End

Chart for How-to Paragraphs

How to _____ -Title
Materials: -Materials
Step 1
Step 2
Step 3 -Steps
Step 4
Step 5

Venn Diagram to Compare and Contrast

Similarities

Item 1   Item 2

Differences

Outlines for Reports

Topic
I. Main Idea
   A. Detail
   B. Detail
   C. Detail
II. Main Idea
   A. Detail
   B. Detail
III. Conclusion

WRITING STRATEGY

Minilesson 61

Introducing Prewriting

Objective: Understand how to use the prewriting handbook pages.

Guiding Question: How do I use these pages to help me come up with ideas for my writing?

Teach/Model

Have students read p. 74. Explain that the steps on this page show how a student begins a persuasive essay by determining the TAP, brainstorming a list of ideas, choosing one idea, and gathering information.

Practice/Apply

Have students discuss making lists, clustering, using a journal, and other ways that they can brainstorm ideas.

Minilesson 62

Organizing Information

Objective: Understand how to use a graphic organizer to put information in order.

Guiding Question: How can I use a graphic organizer to arrange information?

Teach/Model

Explain to students that they can fill in a graphic organizer to arrange information. Point out how the writer listed the main idea and added details in the idea-support map on p. 74.

Practice/Apply

Have students look at the graphic organizers on p. 75. Discuss how they can use each graphic organizer to arrange information for different purposes.

Drafting

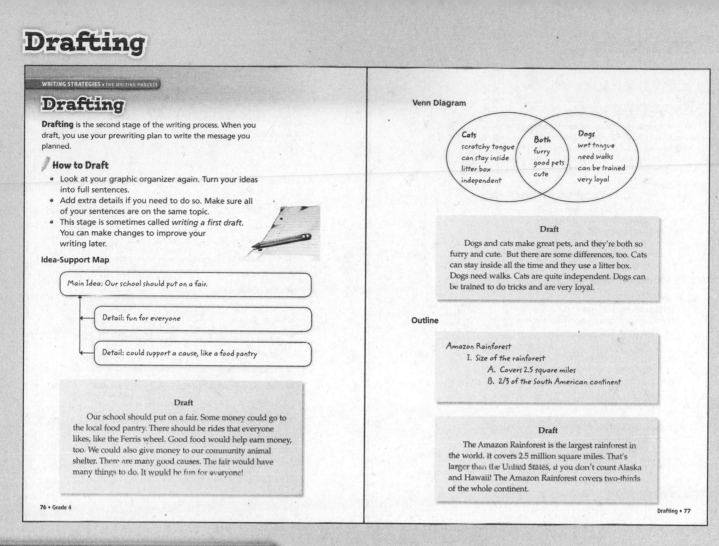

Drafting

Drafting is the second stage of the writing process. When you draft, you use your prewriting plan to write the message you planned.

How to Draft

- Look at your graphic organizer again. Turn your ideas into full sentences.
- Add extra details if you need to do so. Make sure all of your sentences are on the same topic.
- This stage is sometimes called *writing a first draft*. You can make changes to improve your writing later.

Idea-Support Map

Main Idea: Our school should put on a fair.

Detail: fun for everyone

Detail: could support a cause, like a food pantry

Draft

Our school should put on a fair. Some money could go to the local food pantry. There should be rides that everyone likes, like the Ferris wheel. Good food would help earn money, too. We could also give money to our community animal shelter. There are many good causes. The fair would have many things to do. It would be fun for everyone!

76 • Grade 4

Venn Diagram

Cats
scratchy tongue
can stay inside
litter box
independent

Both
furry
good pets
cute

Dogs
wet tongue
need walks
can be trained
very loyal

Draft

Dogs and cats make great pets, and they're both so furry and cute. But there are some differences, too. Cats can stay inside all the time and they use a litter box. Dogs need walks. Cats are quite independent. Dogs can be trained to do tricks and are very loyal.

Outline

Amazon Rainforest
  I. Size of the rainforest
      A. Covers 2.5 square miles
      B. 2/3 of the South American continent

Draft

The Amazon Rainforest is the largest rainforest in the world. It covers 2.5 million square miles. That's larger than the United States, if you don't count Alaska and Hawaii! The Amazon Rainforest covers two-thirds of the whole continent.

Drafting • 77

Minilesson 63

Introducing Drafting

Objective: Understand how to use the drafting handbook pages.

Guiding Question: How do I use these pages to help me start writing?

Teach/Model

Have students read p. 76. Explain that the example on this page shows how a student used the prewriting graphic organizer to write the first draft of a persuasive essay.

Practice/Apply

Have students read the examples on p. 77. Discuss how the examples show two more ways students can use their graphic organizers to write their drafts.

Minilesson 64

Going from Organizer to Draft

Objective: Understand how to use a graphic organizer to draft.

Guiding Question: How can I use my prewriting plan draft?

Teach/Model

Explain to students that one way to start a rough draft is to review the information in their graphic organizer and then write a topic sentence. Then they can follow that first sentence with details. Point out how the writer did this for the Venn diagram. Remind them that they can revise later.

Practice/Apply

Have students discuss how the student used the information in the outline to write a topic sentence and then begin drafting details as support.

Revising

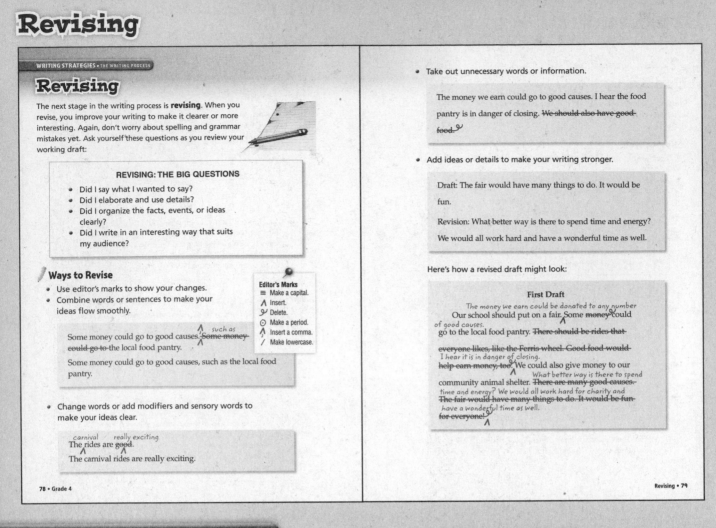

Revising

The next stage in the writing process is **revising**. When you revise, you improve your writing to make it clearer or more interesting. Again, don't worry about spelling and grammar mistakes yet. Ask yourself these questions as you review your working draft:

REVISING: THE BIG QUESTIONS

- Did I say what I wanted to say?
- Did I elaborate and use details?
- Did I organize the facts, events, or ideas clearly?
- Did I write in an interesting way that suits my audience?

Ways to Revise

- Use editor's marks to show your changes.
- Combine words or sentences to make your ideas flow smoothly.

Editor's Marks
≡ Make a capital.
∧ Insert.
❾ Delete.
⊙ Make a period.
∧ Insert a comma.
/ Make lowercase.

Some money could go to good causes. Some money could go to the local food pantry.

Some money could go to good causes, such as the local food pantry.

- Change words or add modifiers and sensory words to make your ideas clear.

The rides are good.

The carnival rides are really exciting.

- Take out unnecessary words or information.

The money we earn could go to good causes. I hear the food pantry is in danger of closing. We should also have good food.

- Add ideas or details to make your writing stronger.

Draft: The fair would have many things to do. It would be fun.

Revision: What better way is there to spend time and energy? We would all work hard and have a wonderful time as well.

Here's how a revised draft might look:

First Draft
The money we earn could be donated to any number
Our school should put on a fair. Some money could
of good causes.
go to the local food pantry. There should be rides that
everyone likes, like the Ferris wheel. Good food would
I hear it is in danger of closing.
help earn money, too. We could also give money to our
What better way is there to spend
community animal shelter. There are many good causes.
time and energy? We would all work hard for charity and
The fair would have many things to do. It would be fun
have a wonderful time as well.
for everyone!

Minilesson 65

Introducing Revising

Objective: Understand how to use the revising handbook pages.

Guiding Question: How do I use these pages to help me revise my writing?

Teach/Model

Have students read p. 78. Explain that the examples on this page show how a student revised parts of a persuasive essay by combining two sentences, adding a modifier, and changing the word *good*.

Practice/Apply

Have students read the examples on p. 79. Discuss how these examples show two more ways students can revise to improve their drafts.

Minilesson 66

Using Editor's Marks

Objective: Understand how to use editor's marks to revise a draft.

Guiding Question: How can I use editor's marks to show changes I want to make?

Teach/Model

Explain to students that they can use editor's marks to show changes as they revise a draft. Have them review the chart on p. 78. Then point out two editor's marks that a student uses in the revised first draft.

Practice/Apply

Have students discuss what the student has added, taken out, changed, or combined to revise the persuasive essay draft.

Editing and Publishing

Editing

Editing, or proofreading for errors, is the fourth stage of the writing process.

Editing

- Check for mistakes in punctuation, capitalization, spelling, and grammar. You can use a dictionary and a grammar book to help.
- Make sure your paragraphs are indented.
- Use editing marks to show corrections on your paper.
- Use the spelling and grammar checker if you are working on a computer. Be sure to double-check your work for errors the checker won't catch.

Editor's Marks
≡ Make a capital.
∧ Insert.
⌿ Delete.
⊙ Make a period.
∧ Insert a comma.
/ Make lowercase.

Revised Draft

Dear Principal Martinez,

The key to a great ~~fair~~ *fair* is good food and ~~exsiting~~ *exciting* rides. That's what makes people come out and spend money⊙

Our school could rent a Ferris wheel∧ a giant slide, and maybe some other rides, too. we could pay back the rental fees from the money ~~erned~~ *earned* at the fair. Food would be easy. Students and parents could work together to make ~~delishus~~ *delicious* food to sell. As you can see, I don't think rides or food for the fair would be a problem.

Sincerely,
Amanda

Publishing

The last stage of the writing process is **publishing**. Before you publish, you can go back to any stage to fix or improve your writing.

- Decide how you want to publish. You might publish by sharing a written piece, giving an oral report, or giving a multimedia presentation.
- Type or write a clean copy of your piece.
- When you give a presentation, write note cards with the main ideas to guide your oral reporting or multimedia presentation.
- If you use multimedia, use a computer to choose pictures, charts, audio, or video to go with your writing.

Why We Should Have a School Fair
by Amanda Fleming

I believe our school should put on a fair. The money we earn could be donated to any number of good causes. Some could go to the local food pantry. We could also give money to our community animal shelter. I hear they're in danger of closing. What better way is there to spend our time and energy? We would be learning a lot about planning, budgets, and cooperating as a school. Just think, we would all be working hard for charity while having a wonderful time!

Minilesson 67

Introducing Editing

Objective: Understand how to use the editing and publishing handbook pages.

Guiding Question: How do I use these pages to check my writing for mistakes?

Teach/Model

Have students read p. 80. Explain that the example on this page shows how Amanda checked for mistakes and then used editor's marks to show corrections in her revised draft.

Practice/Apply

Have students discuss the mistakes in punctuation, capitalization, spelling, and grammar that Amanda caught in her revised draft.

Minilesson 68

Introducing Publishing

Objective: Understand how to use the editing and publishing handbook pages.

Guiding Question: How do I publish my writing?

Teach/Model

Have students read p. 81. Point out that Amanda's persuasive essay is now polished and ready to be published. Explain that there are several ways to publish a piece of writing.

Practice/Apply

Have students discuss how Amanda might decide to publish her edited persuasive essay.

Evidence

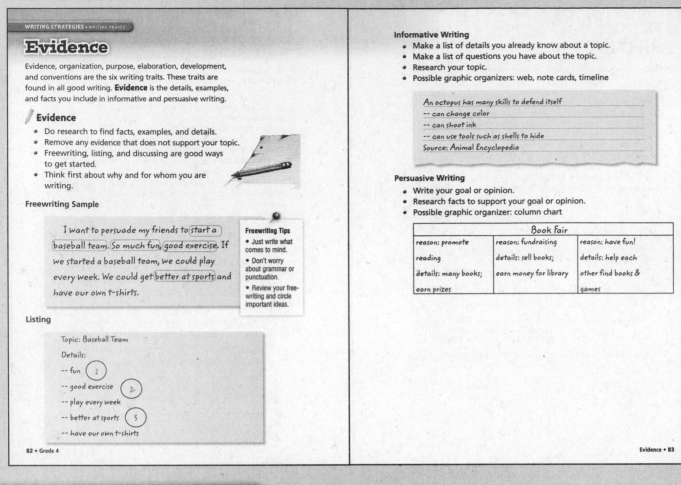

Evidence

Evidence, organization, purpose, elaboration, development, and conventions are the six writing traits. These traits are found in all good writing. **Evidence** is the details, examples, and facts you include in informative and persuasive writing.

Evidence

- Do research to find facts, examples, and details.
- Remove any evidence that does not support your topic.
- Freewriting, listing, and discussing are good ways to get started.
- Think first about why and for whom you are writing.

Freewriting Sample

I want to persuade my friends to start a baseball team. So much fun, good exercise. If we started a baseball team, we could play every week. We could get better at sports and have our own t-shirts.

Freewriting Tips
- Just write what comes to mind.
- Don't worry about grammar or punctuation.
- Review your freewriting and circle important ideas.

Listing

Topic: Baseball Team
Details:
-- fun ①
-- good exercise ②
-- play every week
-- better at sports ③
-- have our own t-shirts

Informative Writing
- Make a list of details you already know about a topic.
- Make a list of questions you have about the topic.
- Research your topic.
- Possible graphic organizers: web, note cards, timeline

An octopus has many skills to defend itself
-- can change color
-- can shoot ink
-- can use tools such as shells to hide
Source: Animal Encyclopedia

Persuasive Writing
- Write your goal or opinion.
- Research facts to support your goal or opinion.
- Possible graphic organizer: column chart

Book Fair		
reason: promote reading	reason: fundraising	reason: have fun!
details: many books; earn prizes	details: sell books; earn money for library	details: help each other find books & games

Minilesson 69

Introducing Evidence

Objective: Understand how to locate evidence to support a topic.

Guiding Question: How do I think of facts, details, and examples to support my topic?

Teach/Model

Have students read p. 82. Explain that the examples on this page show how a student used freewriting and listing to collect evidence about starting a baseball team. Point out the freewriting tips in the box and discuss them.

Practice/Apply

Have students use freewriting or listing to think of topics and evidence for a piece of writing about a hobby they enjoy, like playing soccer.

Minilesson 70

Finding Topics for Different Kinds of Writing

Objective: Find topics for different forms of writing.

Guiding Question: What topics should I think about for informative or persuasive writing?

Teach/Model

Have students read p. 83. For each form of writing, discuss which graphic organizers they might want to use and what topics they will think about or find evidence for.

Practice/Apply

Have students think about topics and evidence for a piece of informative or persuasive writing.

Organization

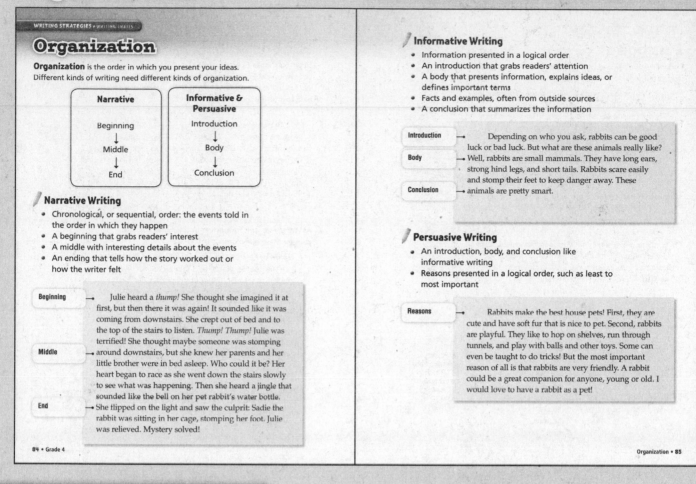

Organization

Organization

Organization is the order in which you present your ideas. Different kinds of writing need different kinds of organization.

Narrative

Beginning
↓
Middle
↓
End

Informative & Persuasive

Introduction
↓
Body
↓
Conclusion

Narrative Writing

- Chronological, or sequential, order: the events told in the order in which they happen
- A beginning that grabs readers' interest
- A middle with interesting details about the events
- An ending that tells how the story worked out or how the writer felt

Beginning → Julie heard a *thump!* She thought she imagined it at first, but then there it was again! It sounded like it was coming from downstairs. She crept out of bed and to the top of the stairs to listen. *Thump! Thump!* Julie was terrified! She thought maybe someone was stomping

Middle → around downstairs, but she knew her parents and her little brother were in bed asleep. Who could it be? Her heart began to race as she went down the stairs slowly to see what was happening. Then she heard a jingle that sounded like the bell on her pet rabbit's water bottle.

End → She flipped on the light and saw the culprit: Sadie the rabbit was sitting in her cage, stomping her foot. Julie was relieved. Mystery solved!

84 • Grade 4

Informative Writing

- Information presented in a logical order
- An introduction that grabs readers' attention
- A body that presents information, explains ideas, or defines important terms
- Facts and examples, often from outside sources
- A conclusion that summarizes the information

Introduction →
Body →
Conclusion →

Depending on who you ask, rabbits can be good luck or bad luck. But what are these animals really like? Well, rabbits are small mammals. They have long ears, strong hind legs, and short tails. Rabbits scare easily and stomp their feet to keep danger away. These animals are pretty smart.

Persuasive Writing

- An introduction, body, and conclusion like informative writing
- Reasons presented in a logical order, such as least to most important

Reasons → Rabbits make the best house pets! First, they are cute and have soft fur that is nice to pet. Second, rabbits are playful. They like to hop on shelves, run through tunnels, and play with balls and other toys. Some can even be taught to do tricks! But the most important reason of all is that rabbits are very friendly. A rabbit could be a great companion for anyone, young or old. I would love to have a rabbit as a pet!

Organization • 85

WRITING STRATEGY

Minilesson 71

Organizing Narrative Writing

Objective: Understand how to organize narrative writing.

Guiding Question: How do I present my ideas in narrative writing?

Teach/Model

Have students read p. 84. Emphasize that different forms of writing have different kinds of organization. Point out that the example of narrative writing on this page tells about events in the order in which they happen.

Practice/Apply

Have students discuss what happens in the beginning, middle, and ending in the example.

Minilesson 72

Organizing Informative and Persuasive Writing

Objective: Understand how to organize informative and persuasive writing.

Guiding Question: How do I present my ideas in informative and persuasive writing?

Teach/Model

Have students read p. 85. Point out that both examples include an introduction, a body, and a conclusion.

Practice/Apply

Guide students to fill in a Venn diagram about the similarities and differences between the organization of the two examples.

Purpose and Elaboration

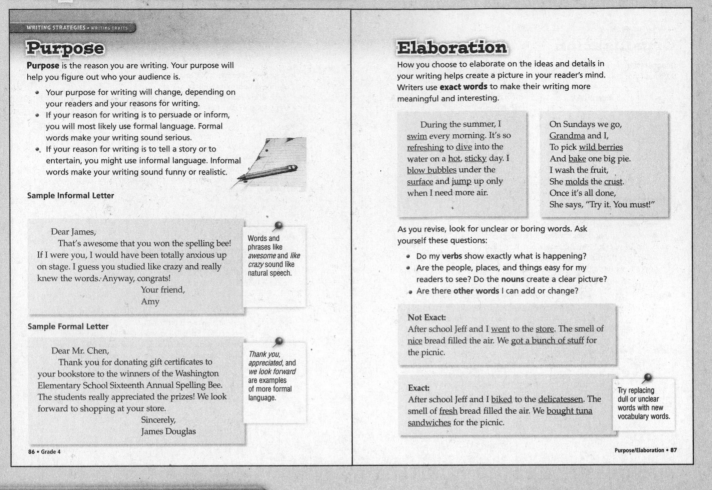

Purpose

Purpose is the reason you are writing. Your purpose will help you figure out who your audience is.

- Your purpose for writing will change, depending on your readers and your reasons for writing.
- If your reason for writing is to persuade or inform, you will most likely use formal language. Formal words make your writing sound serious.
- If your reason for writing is to tell a story or to entertain, you might use informal language. Informal words make your writing sound funny or realistic.

Sample Informal Letter

Dear James,
    That's awesome that you won the spelling bee! If I were you, I would have been totally anxious up on stage. I guess you studied like crazy and really knew the words. Anyway, congrats!
                    Your friend,
                    Amy

Words and phrases like *awesome* and *like crazy* sound like natural speech.

Sample Formal Letter

Dear Mr. Chen,
    Thank you for donating gift certificates to your bookstore to the winners of the Washington Elementary School Sixteenth Annual Spelling Bee. The students really appreciated the prizes! We look forward to shopping at your store.
                    Sincerely,
                    James Douglas

Thank you, appreciated, and *we look forward* are examples of more formal language.

86 • Grade 4

Elaboration

How you choose to elaborate on the ideas and details in your writing helps create a picture in your reader's mind. Writers use **exact words** to make their writing more meaningful and interesting.

During the summer, I <u>swim</u> every morning. It's so <u>refreshing</u> to <u>dive</u> into the water on a <u>hot</u>, <u>sticky</u> day. I <u>blow bubbles</u> under the <u>surface</u> and <u>jump</u> up only when I need more air.

On Sundays we go, <u>Grandma</u> and I, To pick <u>wild berries</u> And <u>bake</u> one big pie. I wash the fruit, She <u>molds</u> the <u>crust</u>. Once it's all done, She says, "Try it. You must!"

As you revise, look for unclear or boring words. Ask yourself these questions:

- Do my **verbs** show exactly what is happening?
- Are the people, places, and things easy for my readers to see? Do the **nouns** create a clear picture?
- Are there **other words** I can add or change?

Not Exact:
After school Jeff and I <u>went</u> to the <u>store</u>. The smell of <u>nice</u> bread filled the air. We <u>got a bunch of stuff</u> for the picnic.

Exact:
After school Jeff and I <u>biked</u> to the <u>delicatessen</u>. The smell of <u>fresh</u> bread filled the air. We <u>bought tuna sandwiches</u> for the picnic.

Try replacing dull or unclear words with new vocabulary words.

Purpose/Elaboration • 87

WRITING STRATEGY

Minilesson 73

Understanding Purpose

Objective: Understand that the purpose for writing will determine when to use formal or informal language.

Guiding Question: How do I decide whether to use formal or informal language in my writing?

Teach/Model

Have students read p. 86. Explain that Amy and James use different styles of language in the examples. Discuss the purpose each writer has for writing. Point out that Amy uses informal language in the first letter, but James uses formal language in the second letter.

Practice/Apply

Have students identify the writers' purposes in each letter and why informal or formal language was used.

Minilesson 74

Understanding Elaboration

Objective: Understand how to elaborate using exact words.

Guiding Question: How can I make my writing clear and interesting?

Teach/Model

Have students read p. 87. Explain that exact words help create a picture in a reader's mind. Point out the underlined nouns, verbs, and adjectives in the two examples on this page.

Practice/Apply

Have students discuss how the writer replaced the underlined words in the first passage at the bottom of the page with more specific words. Challenge students to think of other exact words the writer may have used.

Development

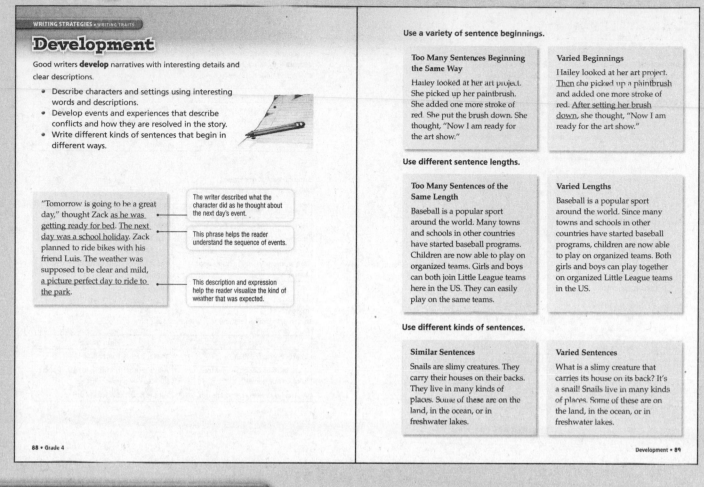

Development

Good writers **develop** narratives with interesting details and clear descriptions.

- Describe characters and settings using interesting words and descriptions.
- Develop events and experiences that describe conflicts and how they are resolved in the story.
- Write different kinds of sentences that begin in different ways.

"Tomorrow is going to be a great day," thought Zack <u>as he was getting ready for bed. The next day was a school holiday.</u> Zack planned to ride bikes with his friend Luis. The weather was supposed to be clear and mild, <u>a picture perfect day to ride to the park.</u>

The writer described what the character did as he thought about the next day's event.

This phrase helps the reader understand the sequence of events.

This description and expression help the reader visualize the kind of weather that was expected.

Use a variety of sentence beginnings.

Too Many Sentences Beginning the Same Way

Hailey looked at her art project. She picked up her paintbrush. She added one more stroke of red. She put the brush down. She thought, "Now I am ready for the art show."

Varied Beginnings

Hailey looked at her art project. Then she picked up a paintbrush and added one more stroke of red. <u>After setting her brush down,</u> she thought, "Now I am ready for the art show."

Use different sentence lengths.

Too Many Sentences of the Same Length

Baseball is a popular sport around the world. Many towns and schools in other countries have started baseball programs. Children are now able to play on organized teams. Girls and boys can both join Little League teams here in the US. They can easily play on the same teams.

Varied Lengths

Baseball is a popular sport around the world. Since many towns and schools in other countries have started baseball programs, children are now able to play on organized teams. Both girls and boys can play together on organized Little League teams in the US.

Use different kinds of sentences.

Similar Sentences

Snails are slimy creatures. They carry their houses on their backs. They live in many kinds of places. Some of these are on the land, in the ocean, or in freshwater lakes.

Varied Sentences

What is a slimy creature that carries its house on its back? It's a snail! Snails live in many kinds of places. Some of these are on the land, in the ocean, or in freshwater lakes.

Minilesson 75

Understanding Development

Objective: Understand how to develop good narratives.

Guiding Question: How do I make narratives interesting and easy to understand?

Teach/Model

Have students read the top of p. 88. Explain that good writers do more than just list a sequence of events when they write a story. Instead they add details and descriptions that help readers understand why the characters act as they do.

Practice/Apply

Have students read the model on p. 88. Discuss how the underlined text gives readers information about the story and helps to make the story more interesting to read.

Minilesson 76

Using Sentence Variety

Objective: Understand how to develop sentences that vary.

Guiding Question: How can I vary my sentences to make my writing more interesting?

Teach/Model

Have students read p. 89. Explain that the three pairs of examples show different ways to vary sentences. Point out how writers can use different sentence beginnings, a mix of short and long sentences, and different kinds of sentences to make readers want to continue reading.

Practice/Apply

Have students develop three related sentences about a topic. Remind them to develop sentences that are varied and that include interesting words and details.

Conventions

Conventions

Conventions are rules about grammar, spelling, punctuation, and capitalization. One way to make sure you are following the rules when you write or edit is to have an editing checklist.

Sample Editing Checklist

> **Punctuation**
> ___ Did I use correct end punctuation in my sentences?
> ___ Did I use commas correctly in compound sentences?
> ___ Did I use quotation marks correctly?
> **Capitalization**
> ___ Did I start every sentence with a capital letter?
> ___ Did I capitalize proper nouns?
> **Spelling**
> ___ Did I spell all of my words correctly?
> **Grammar**
> ___ Did my sentences have correct subject-verb agreement?
> ___ Did I avoid run-on sentences and fragments?

Common Errors

Fragments and Run-Ons
A sentence should have a **subject** and a **verb**. It starts with a capital letter and ends with a period.

Wrong Way	Right Way
The sheep in the field.	The sheep in the field are ready to be sheared.
Can shear them to gather the wool.	The farmers can shear them to gather the wool.
Wool made from sheep was one of the first textiles people around the world make clothing from wool.	Wool made from sheep was one of the first textiles. People around the world make clothing from wool.

Compound and Complex Sentences
A **compound sentence** combines two sentences. The clauses are separated by a comma and a coordinating conjunction. A **complex sentence** has an independent and a dependent clause and does not need a comma.

Wrong Way	Right Way
The barn is only half-painted but it already looks great!	The barn is only half-painted, but it already looks great!
The cows are fed, after they are milked.	The cows are fed after they are milked.

Subject-Verb Agreement
Make sure the subject and verb of your sentence agree.

Wrong Way	Right Way
Joan plant tree in the schoolyard.	Joan plants a tree in the schoolyard.
José and Marisol paints a mural near the playground.	José and Marisol paint a mural near the playground.
The students wants to make recess better.	The students want to make recess better.

Possessives
Use an apostrophe to show that a noun is possessive.

Wrong Way	Right Way
That is Barrys football.	That is Barry's football.
Alexs mother brings sandwiches and juice to our game's.	Alex's mother brings sandwiches and juice to our games.
All the boy's new jerseys are red.	All the boys' new jerseys are red.

Minilesson 77

Using an Editing Checklist

Objective: Follow rules about grammar, spelling, punctuation, and capitalization.

Guiding Question: How do I use an editing checklist to improve my writing?

Teach/Model

Have students read p. 90. Explain that the checklist shows the kinds of errors that a writer looks for when writing or editing a draft.

Practice/Apply

Using the editing checklist, have students review drafts of their own writing to make sure they have followed these rules.

Minilesson 78

Understanding Common Errors

Objective: Understand common mistakes in writing.

Guiding Question: What mistakes should I look for when I edit my writing?

Teach/Model

Have students read the examples of common errors in the charts on pp. 90–91. Discuss grammar and punctuation mistakes that are illustrated in each chart.

Practice/Apply

Have students check their own writing to make sure they have written sentences with a subject and a verb, used correct subject-verb agreement, and correctly punctuated compound or complex sentences and possessives.

Writing Workshop

Writing Workshop

In a **writing workshop**, writers read each other's work. Then they ask questions about the work or suggest changes. The goal of a workshop is to make everyone's writing better.

How a Writing Workshop Works

- Give everyone a copy of your revised draft.
- Read your writing aloud, or have everyone in the group read silently.
- Listen attentively and take notes.
- Point out the good qualities in your classmates' work.
- Ask questions if something is confusing.
- Politely and respectfully suggest ways to improve writing.

I know we have to make up extra snow days. I think we should make them up during spring break instead of in June. Making up days during spring break will keep students focused. Also, we will still get a few days to relax. Spring break is great, but getting out of school early in June is better. Summer already seems too short. If we have to make up three days, that is actually five more days of June spent in school. Please consider changing the make-up policy. Students will thank you.

> Add a transition word—maybe however.

> What do you mean by focused?

> What makes getting out early in June "better"?

> How do 3 make-up days turn into 5?

> Your paragraph is organized well!

Guide for a Writing Workshop

The Writer's Job

- ☐ Give a copy of your writing to each of the classmates in your workshop.
- ☐ Read your paper aloud or introduce your writing and let classmates read it silently.
- ☐ Ask for comments and listen carefully. Keep an open mind.
- ☐ Take notes or write down suggestions to help you remember.
- ☐ Ask for advice about anything you had trouble with.
- ☐ Reread your paper after the workshop.
- ☐ Use your notes to revise and make changes.

The Responder's Job

- ☐ Be kind, respectful, positive, polite, and helpful.
- ☐ Listen to or read the writing carefully.
- ☐ Make notes about the writing.
- ☐ Retell what you have heard.
- ☐ Tell at least two things that you liked about the writing. Be specific.
- ☐ Ask questions about things you don't understand.
- ☐ Give one or two suggestions to help the writer.

Negative/Unhelpful Responses	Positive/Helpful Responses
Why are your details so dull?	What exciting details could you add?
Where's the ending?	What new way can you end the story?
Why didn't you tell more about your character?	What is your character like?

WRITING STRATEGY

Minilesson 79

Understanding the Writing Workshop

Objective: Understand how a writing workshop works.

Guiding Question: How can a writing workshop help improve my writing?

Teach/Model

Have students read p. 92. Review the bulleted steps. Explain that the example shows how a student points out strengths and weaknesses in a classmate's writing.

Practice/Apply

Have students discuss the comments made by the workshop reader in the example on this page. Ask if they agree or disagree with the comments and why.

Minilesson 80

Using a Workshop Checklist

Objective: Use a checklist as a guide for a writing workshop.

Guiding Question: In a writing workshop, what is the writer's job? What is the responder's job?

Teach/Model

Have students read p. 93. Explain that these checklists will guide them in a writing workshop. Point out that the first list guides the writer, while the second list guides student readers who respond to a piece of writing.

Practice/Apply

Have students hold a writing workshop using the two checklists and the chart on this page to offer helpful responses.

Using the Internet

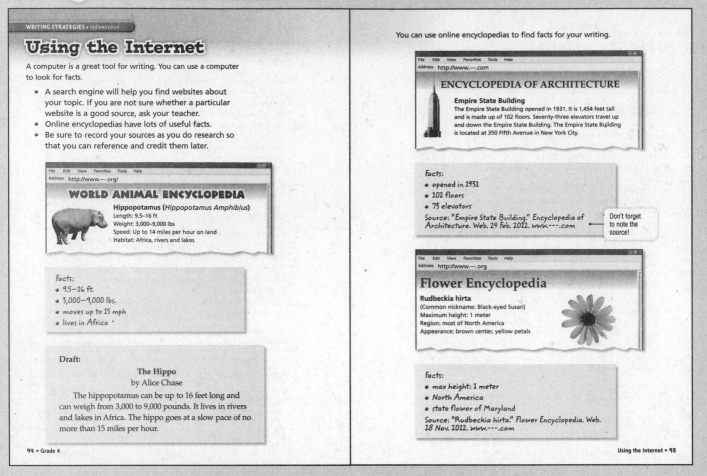

WRITING STRATEGIES • TECHNOLOGY

Using the Internet

A computer is a great tool for writing. You can use a computer to look for facts.

- A search engine will help you find websites about your topic. If you are not sure whether a particular website is a good source, ask your teacher.
- Online encyclopedias have lots of useful facts.
- Be sure to record your sources as you do research so that you can reference and credit them later.

File   Edit   View   Favorites   Tools   Help
Address http://www.---.org/

WORLD ANIMAL ENCYCLOPEDIA

Hippopotamus (*Hippopotamus Amphibius*)
Length: 9.5–16 ft
Weight: 3,000–9,000 lbs
Speed: Up to 14 miles per hour on land
Habitat: Africa, rivers and lakes

Facts:
- 9.5–16 ft.
- 3,000–9,000 lbs.
- moves up to 15 mph
- lives in Africa

Draft:

The Hippo
by Alice Chase

The hippopotamus can be up to 16 feet long and can weigh from 3,000 to 9,000 pounds. It lives in rivers and lakes in Africa. The hippo goes at a slow pace of no more than 15 miles per hour.

94 • Grade 4

You can use online encyclopedias to find facts for your writing.

File   Edit   View   Favorites   Tools   Help
Address http://www.---.com

ENCYCLOPEDIA OF ARCHITECTURE

Empire State Building
The Empire State Building opened in 1931. It is 1,454 feet tall and is made up of 102 floors. Seventy-three elevators travel up and down the Empire State Building. The Empire State Building is located at 350 Fifth Avenue in New York City.

Facts:
- opened in 1931
- 102 floors
- 73 elevators

Source: "Empire State Building." Encyclopedia of Architecture. Web. 24 Feb. 2012. www.---.com

Don't forget to note the source!

File   Edit   View   Favorites   Tools   Help
Address http://www.---.org

Flower Encyclopedia

Rudbeckia hirta
(Common nickname: Black-eyed Susan)
Maximum height: 1 meter
Region: most of North America
Appearance: brown center, yellow petals

Facts:
- max height: 1 meter
- North America
- state flower of Maryland

Source: "Rudbeckia hirta." Flower Encyclopedia. Web. 28 Nov. 2012. www.---.com

Using the Internet • 95

WRITING STRATEGY

Minilesson 81

Using the Internet for Writing

Objective: Understand how to use the Internet to find facts.

Guiding Question: How do I use the Internet for my writing?

Teach/Model

Have students read p. 94. Explain that they can use the Internet to find websites or online encyclopedias to learn about a topic. Point out that the example on this page shows how Alice used an online encyclopedia to draft an informational paragraph about hippos.

Practice/Apply

Ask students which search engines, websites, and online encyclopedias they have used to look for facts. List examples on the board. Guide them to understand which examples are reliable sources of information.

Minilesson 82

Using Online Encyclopedias

Objective: Understand how to use an online encyclopedia.

Guiding Question: How can I use an online encyclopedia to find facts?

Teach/Model

Explain to students that one way to find facts for their writing is by using an online encyclopedia. Have them read the examples on p. 95. Point out how a student found facts using the Encyclopedia of Architecture and the Flower Encyclopedia.

Practice/Apply

Have students use an online encyclopedia to find three facts about a planet, an inventor, or an animal in the rainforest. Remind them to record their sources.

Writing for the Web

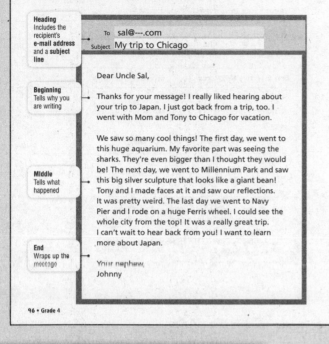

TECHNOLOGY · WRITING FOR THE WEB

Writing for the Web

There are many ways to use technology to write. One way is to write for the web.

E-mail

You can send an e-mail to a friend or family member. It can also be sent for business purposes, which requires more formal language. An e-mail is a lot like a friendly letter. You can write an e-mail to connect with anyone around the world.

Heading
Includes the recipient's **e-mail address** and a **subject line**

To sal@---.com
Subject My trip to Chicago

Beginning
Tells why you are writing

Dear Uncle Sal,

Thanks for your message! I really liked hearing about your trip to Japan. I just got back from a trip, too. I went with Mom and Tony to Chicago for vacation.

Middle
Tells what happened

We saw so many cool things! The first day, we went to this huge aquarium. My favorite part was seeing the sharks. They're even bigger than I thought they would be! The next day, we went to Millennium Park and saw this big silver sculpture that looks like a giant bean! Tony and I made faces at it and saw our reflections. It was pretty weird. The last day we went to Navy Pier and I rode on a huge Ferris wheel. I could see the whole city from the top! It was a really great trip. I can't wait to hear back from you! I want to learn more about Japan.

End
Wraps up the message

Your nephew,
Johnny

96 • Grade 4

Blog Post

Blog is short for "weblog." It is a journal that you keep on the Internet so that other people can read and comment. One way to use a blog is to share news about yourself or your friends and family with others. Blogs can also be essays or include opinions.

URL

Blog Name

Post Title

File Edit View Favorites Tools Help
Address http://www.---.com/blog

Mrs. Appletree's 4th Grade Class Blog

→Big news in our classroom!
→by Jake on November 13, 2012 at 1:33pm

Byline
Tells who wrote the post and when it was published

There is lots of big news in Mrs. Appletree's class! Three students are going to the State Science Fair in January. Lisa, Andre, and Michael will go to the Fair to present the robot they made. The robot can pick up pencils!

Body
Tells what happened or gives thoughts and feelings

Melissa and Gabriela both made the girl's basketball team this fall. They will be playing against the kids from Pembroke Elementary on Friday. We know they're going to win. Go Bears!

Mei, Garrett, and Luisa each got a special award from the school for reading ten books each in this month's reading challenge. They each won gift certificates to a local bookstore. They're going to need plenty more books if they keep reading this way!

Comments
Left by readers

Comments
→Mrs. Appletree
Way to go Lisa, Andre, Michael, Melissa, Gabriel, Mei, Garrett, and Luisa! Thanks for making this such a great class to teach!

Writing for the Web • 97

WRITING STRATEGY

Minilesson 83

Writing an E-mail

Objective: Understand how to write an e-mail.

Guiding Question: How do I write an e-mail to friends or family members?

Teach/Model

Have students read p. 96. Explain that the example on this page shows Johnny's e-mail to his Uncle Sal. Referring to the call-outs, discuss the format of an e-mail.

Practice/Apply

Have students use a computer to write an e-mail to a friend or family member. Remind them that an e-mail is similar to a friendly letter.

Minilesson 84

Writing a Blog Post

Objective: Understand how to write a blog post.

Guiding Question: What are the key parts of a blog post?

Teach/Model

Have students read p. 97. Explain that the example on this page shows how a blog post is set up and what elements it includes. Point out the call-outs, and discuss each one. Have students tell who wrote the blog post and what the post is about.

Practice/Apply

Help students use a computer to create a blog post about their own class. Remind them to include a blog name, a post title, a byline, and a body that tells what happened or shares their thoughts and feelings.

Doing Research
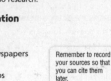

WRITING STRATEGIES

Doing Research

The best way to support your points in your informative or persuasive writing is to use facts and details. The best way to find facts and details is to do research.

Sources of Information

- Books
- Encyclopedias
- Magazines and Newspapers
- The Internet
- Television and Videos
- Interviews

> Remember to record your sources so that you can cite them later.

Evaluating Sources

Some sources are better than others or have more reliable information. How can you tell which sources are good? When looking at a new source, ask yourself these questions:

- ☐ Is the source published by an institution, organization, or person who knows the subject well?
- ☐ If it is a website, is it trustworthy? (Sites with *.edu*, *.org*, or *.gov* are usually educational, nonprofit, or government websites and can have good information.)
- ☐ Is there background information in the author's biography or author's website?
- ☐ Is the source up to date?
- ☐ Is the purpose or point of view of the source stated? If there is more than one side to the issue, are both sides presented?
- ☐ Is the information complete?

Finding Information

One way to find information is to search in your library's electronic card catalog or use an Internet search engine. In order to find good sources of information, you need to search using good keywords.

A **keyword** is a word or phrase about a subject. A good keyword to start with might be the topic of your research.

Tips:

- Narrow your topic down to a specific keyword. If you pick something too broad, your search will get hundreds of results.
- Don't pick anything too specific or you won't find enough results to get enough information.

Less Effective Keywords	Effective Keywords
cars	the first car
old cars	Model T
inventors	Henry Ford
Grandma's red 1957 Chevy	1957 Chevys

Parts of a Nonfiction Book

- A **table of contents** shows how the book is organized and lists names and page numbers of chapters
- A **glossary** gives definitions of special words used in the book
- A **bibliography** lists sources the author used when writing the book
- An **index** is an alphabetical list of topics covered in the book

---

WRITING STRATEGY

Minilesson 85

Finding Reliable Sources

Objective: Determine which sources of information are reliable.

Guiding Question: How can I tell whether a source is good?

Teach/Model

Have students read p. 98. Explain that it is important for them to choose a reliable source of information when they are looking for facts and details for their informative or persuasive writing. Point out that the checklist on this page will help them decide whether their sources are good.

Practice/Apply

Refer students to the bulleted list on this page. Have them discuss which sources they have used to find facts and details and how they can evaluate each one.

Minilesson 86

Finding Good Sources of Information

Objective: Understand how to find good sources.

Guiding Question: How do I find good sources of information?

Teach/Model

Have students read p. 99. Explain that choosing effective keywords is one way to find good sources of information. Point out the tips for choosing a keyword. Then discuss how to use the parts of a nonfiction book to find specific facts and details.

Practice/Apply

Have students list several possible keywords for an Internet search on a favorite athlete or other public figure. Help them to narrow their keywords.

Notetaking

Notetaking

You will find a great deal of information when you research. One way to keep track of it and stay organized is to take notes.

Note Cards

You can take notes on your research in two ways.

1. You can write a main idea or a research question at the top of the card. Then write details or the answer to your research question below. At the bottom, include your source.

Main Idea	→ Japanese rhinoceros beetles are popular pets in Japan
Details	→ -- can buy them at many stores, including in vending machines! -- Cost 500-1000 yen, or $5-10 -- often characters in TV shows, movies, and advertisements
Source	Source: Smith, James. Animal Encyclopedia. New York: Children's House, 2011. p. 13

2. You can write your research question at the top and then include a direct quote from the source.

Research Question	→ How big are Japanese rhinoceros beetles?
Direct Quote from Source	"The Japanese rhinoceros beetle is a kind of beetle that can grow to be as large as two and a half inches long."
Source	Source: Healy, Patricia. All About Beetles. Boston: Simpson, 2007. p. 47

Writing to Learn

Think-Aloud on Paper

- As you read, write notes about what you are reading.
- Write notes on what you understand about the topic.
- You might write notes on what images you picture as you read, what you predict will happen in a story, or how what you read is like something you have experienced.

Learning Logs

- A learning log is a place for you to comment on, ask questions about, or make connections to your reading.
- In the "Note-Taking" column, write the exact words you read.
- In the "Note-Making" column, write your reactions to or questions about what you read.

Learning Log: "Starting a Garden"	
Note-Taking	**Note-Making**
"Plant seeds in the spring." "Choose good plants for your garden." "You should see sprouts about ten days after you plant your seeds."	What day is the best day to plant seeds? I want to plant cucumbers and tomatoes. Cucumbers are tasty. Is there anything I can do to make my plants grow faster?

WRITING STRATEGY

Minilesson 87

Taking Notes

Objective: Understand how to take notes.

Guiding Question: How do I take notes when I research information?

Teach/Model

Have students read p. 100. Explain that the examples on this page show two different ways that students used note cards to keep track of information about Japanese rhinoceros beetles.

Practice/Apply

Have students research a different insect, such as a firefly, a praying mantis, or a leafcutter ant. Have them take notes using each method for making note cards.

Minilesson 88

Using a Learning Log

Objective: Understand how to use a learning log.

Guiding Question: How can I use a learning log while I read?

Teach/Model

Have students read p. 101. Explain that one way to take notes while reading is to use a learning log. Point out how a student did this for the topic *starting a garden*.

Practice/Apply

Have individuals practice writing in a learning log as they read a short sample text. Have small groups compare the exact words they quoted in the first column and the reactions they recorded in the second column.

Writing to a Prompt

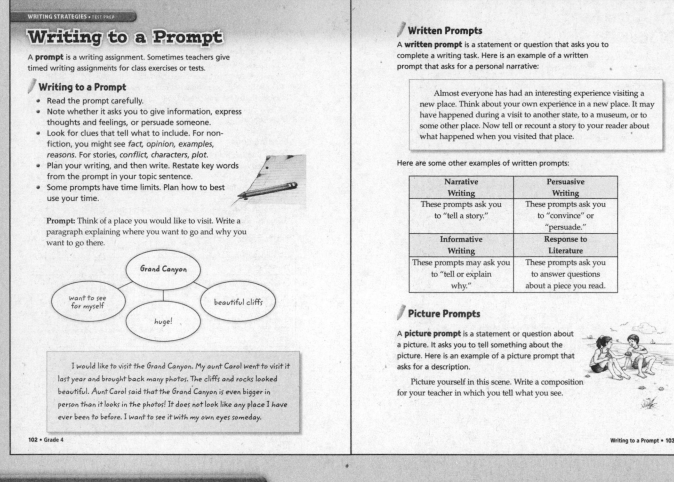

Writing to a Prompt

A **prompt** is a writing assignment. Sometimes teachers give timed writing assignments for class exercises or tests.

Writing to a Prompt

- Read the prompt carefully.
- Note whether it asks you to give information, express thoughts and feelings, or persuade someone.
- Look for clues that tell what to include. For non-fiction, you might see *fact, opinion, examples, reasons*. For stories, *conflict, characters, plot*.
- Plan your writing, and then write. Restate key words from the prompt in your topic sentence.
- Some prompts have time limits. Plan how to best use your time.

Prompt: Think of a place you would like to visit. Write a paragraph explaining where you want to go and why you want to go there.

Grand Canyon

want to see for myself

huge!

beautiful cliffs

I would like to visit the Grand Canyon. My aunt Carol went to visit it last year and brought back many photos. The cliffs and rocks looked beautiful. Aunt Carol said that the Grand Canyon is even bigger in person than it looks in the photos! It does not look like any place I have ever been to before. I want to see it with my own eyes someday.

Written Prompts

A **written prompt** is a statement or question that asks you to complete a writing task. Here is an example of a written prompt that asks for a personal narrative:

> Almost everyone has had an interesting experience visiting a new place. Think about your own experience in a new place. It may have happened during a visit to another state, to a museum, or to some other place. Now tell or recount a story to your reader about what happened when you visited that place.

Here are some other examples of written prompts:

Narrative Writing	Persuasive Writing
These prompts ask you to "tell a story."	These prompts ask you to "convince" or "persuade."
Informative Writing	**Response to Literature**
These prompts may ask you to "tell or explain why."	These prompts ask you to answer questions about a piece you read.

Picture Prompts

A **picture prompt** is a statement or question about a picture. It asks you to tell something about the picture. Here is an example of a picture prompt that asks for a description.

Picture yourself in this scene. Write a composition for your teacher in which you tell what you see.

WRITING STRATEGY

Minilesson 89

Writing to a Prompt

Objective: Understand how to write to a prompt.

Guiding Question: How do I write to a prompt?

Teach/Model

Have students read p. 102. Explain that the example on this page shows how a student wrote to a prompt, using a graphic organizer to plan a personal narrative paragraph. Point out how the student restated key words from the prompt in the topic sentence of the paragraph.

Practice/Apply

Have students use the prompt on this page to write a personal narrative paragraph. Remind them to follow the bulleted list of steps for writing to a prompt.

Minilesson 90

Understanding Different Kinds of Prompts

Objective: Understand different kinds of prompts.

Guiding Question: How do I write to different kinds of prompts?

Teach/Model

Have students read p. 103. Explain that this shows two kinds of prompts: one that is written and one that is a picture. Point out the examples of a written prompt for a personal narrative and the picture prompt for a description. Then discuss the other examples of written prompts in the chart.

Practice/Apply

Have students use the picture prompt on this page to write a short description.

Checklists and Rubrics

EVALUATION

Checklists and Rubrics

A **rubric** is a chart that helps you when you write and revise.
Score 6 tells you what to aim for in your writing.

	• Focus • Support	• Organization
Score 6	My writing is focused and supported by facts or details.	My writing has a clear introduction and conclusion. Ideas are clearly organized.
Score 5	My writing is mostly focused and supported by facts or details.	My writing has an introduction and a conclusion. Ideas are mostly organized.
Score 4	My writing is mostly focused and supported by some facts or details.	My writing has an introduction and a conclusion. Most ideas are organized.
Score 3	Some of my writing is focused and supported by some facts or details.	My writing has an introduction or a conclusion, but might be missing one. Some ideas are organized.
Score 2	My writing is not focused and is supported by few facts or details.	My writing might not have an introduction or a conclusion. Few ideas are organized.
Score 1	My writing is not focused or supported by facts or details.	My writing is missing an introduction and a conclusion. Few or no ideas are organized.

• Elaboration • Purpose	• Conventions • Development • Evidence
Purpose is strong. Writing grabs readers' interest. Word choices strongly support the purpose and audience.	Writing has no errors in spelling, grammar, capitalization, or punctuation. It includes description, details, and/or reasons.
Purpose is clear. Writing holds readers' interest. Most word choices support the purpose and audience.	Writing has few errors in spelling, grammar, capitalization, or punctuation. It includes descriptions, details, and/or reasons.
Purpose is clear, but could be stronger in the beginning or end. Overall writing holds readers' interest. Word choices good.	Writing has some errors in spelling, grammar, capitalization, or punctuation. It includes some description, details, and/or reasons.
Purpose is clear at the beginning or end. Some of the writing interests readers. Few word choices support the purpose and audience.	Writing has some errors in spelling, grammar, capitalization, or punctuation. It includes a few examples of description, details, and/or reasons.
Purpose is mostly unclear. Writing does not include desciption and does not hold readers' interest. Weak word choices.	Writing has many errors in spelling, grammar, capitalization, or punctuation. Little variety of sentences. Some sentences are incomplete.
Purpose is unclear. Writing is not interesting to read.	Writing has many errors in spelling, grammar, capitalization, or punctuation.

WRITING STRATEGY

Minilesson 91

Introducing Rubrics

Objective: Understand what a rubric is and how it is organized.

Guiding Question: What is a rubric, and how is it organized?

Teach/Model

Have students read pp. 104–105. Explain that the rubric on these pages is a chart with four headings across the top and a scoring guide from 6 to 1 down the left side. Tell students that they can use a rubric to determine how well a piece of writing fulfills each listed trait or characteristic.

Practice/Apply

Discuss each of the four headings at the top of the rubric. Have students review the writing traits on handbook pp. 82–90.

Minilesson 92

Using a Rubric to Improve Writing

Objective: Use a rubric to improve a piece of writing.

Guiding Question: How can I use a rubric to improve my writing?

Teach/Model

Model how to use the rubric to assign a score to a writing sample. Explain that students can use a rubric as a guide when revising and editing their writing. A rubric gives them feedback about what improvements need to be made. Remind them that the checklists in the Writing Forms section of the handbook can also help guide the revision process.

Practice/Apply

Have students use the rubric to evaluate a sample of their own writing.

Summary

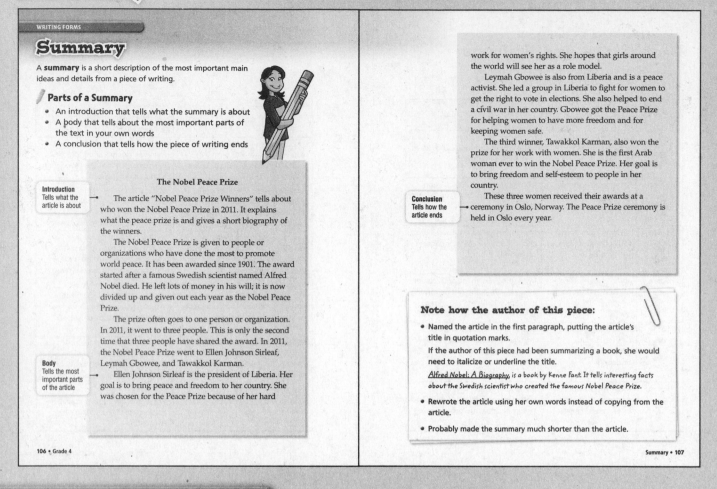

Summary

A **summary** is a short description of the most important main ideas and details from a piece of writing.

Parts of a Summary

- An introduction that tells what the summary is about
- A body that tells about the most important parts of the text in your own words
- A conclusion that tells how the piece of writing ends

Introduction
Tells what the article is about

The Nobel Peace Prize

The article "Nobel Peace Prize Winners" tells about who won the Nobel Peace Prize in 2011. It explains what the peace prize is and gives a short biography of the winners.

The Nobel Peace Prize is given to people or organizations who have done the most to promote world peace. It has been awarded since 1901. The award started after a famous Swedish scientist named Alfred Nobel died. He left lots of money in his will; it is now divided up and given out each year as the Nobel Peace Prize.

The prize often goes to one person or organization. In 2011, it went to three people. This is only the second time that three people have shared the award. In 2011, the Nobel Peace Prize went to Ellen Johnson Sirleaf, Leymah Gbowee, and Tawakkol Karman.

Body
Tells the most important parts of the article

Ellen Johnson Sirleaf is the president of Liberia. Her goal is to bring peace and freedom to her country. She was chosen for the Peace Prize because of her hard work for women's rights. She hopes that girls around the world will see her as a role model.

Leymah Gbowee is also from Liberia and is a peace activist. She led a group in Liberia to fight for women to get the right to vote in elections. She also helped to end a civil war in her country. Gbowee got the Peace Prize for helping women to have more freedom and for keeping women safe.

The third winner, Tawakkol Karman, also won the prize for her work with women. She is the first Arab woman ever to win the Nobel Peace Prize. Her goal is to bring freedom and self-esteem to people in her country.

Conclusion
Tells how the article ends

These three women received their awards at a ceremony in Oslo, Norway. The Peace Prize ceremony is held in Oslo every year.

Note how the author of this piece:

- Named the article in the first paragraph, putting the article's title in quotation marks.

  If the author of this piece had been summarizing a book, she would need to italicize or underline the title.

  Alfred Nobel: A Biography, is a book by Kenne Fant. It tells interesting facts about the Swedish scientist who created the famous Nobel Peace Prize.

- Rewrote the article using her own words instead of copying from the article.

- Probably made the summary much shorter than the article.

WRITING MODELS AND FORMS

Minilesson 93

Understanding the Summary

Objective: Understand the summary.

Guiding Question: How can I use these pages to help me write a good summary?

Teach/Model

Have students read the definition and bulleted points. Explain that the example on these pages is a summary of an article, "Nobel Peace Prize Winners." Then have students read to the end of p. 107.

Practice/Apply

Have students identify the introduction, body, and conclusion of the summary. Discuss what the author tells about the article "Nobel Peace Prize Winners" in each part of her summary.

Minilesson 94

Recognizing Important Details

Objective: Recognize important main ideas and details.

Guiding Question: Which main ideas and details will I include in my summary?

Teach/Model

Explain to students that a summary includes only the main ideas and details that are necessary for readers to understand the original piece of writing. Discuss the main ideas and details the author used in her summary of "Nobel Peace Prize Winners."

Practice/Apply

Have students write a summary of a short nonfiction article they have read. Remind them to include only the most important main ideas and details.

Cause-and-Effect Essay

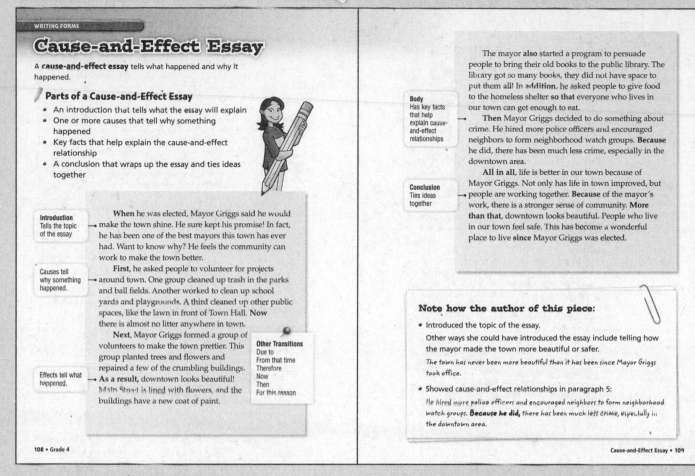

Minilesson 95	Minilesson 96

Understanding Cause and Effect

Objective: Understand the cause-and-effect essay.

Guiding Question: How can I use these pages to help me write a good cause-and-effect essay?

Teach/Model

Have students read the definition and bulleted points. Explain that the example on these pages is a cause-and-effect essay about how Mayor Griggs improved his town. Point out a few examples of how Mayor Griggs's acts changed the town and explain that these are causes and effects.

Practice/Apply

Have students identify cause-and-effect relationships in the essay. On the board, list causes and effects in a T-map.

Using Cause-and-Effect Transitions

Objective: Use cause-and-effect transition words.

Guiding Question: How will I use transition words in my essay to signal cause-and-effect relationships?

Teach/Model

Explain to students that the author of this essay used cause-and-effect transition words to connect ideas clearly. Point out *as a result* in the third paragraph. Discuss the cause-and-effect relationship that this transition signals to the reader.

Practice/Apply

Have students find the words *so that* and *because* in this essay. Have them discuss the cause-and-effect relationships that these transitions signal.

Problem/Solution Composition

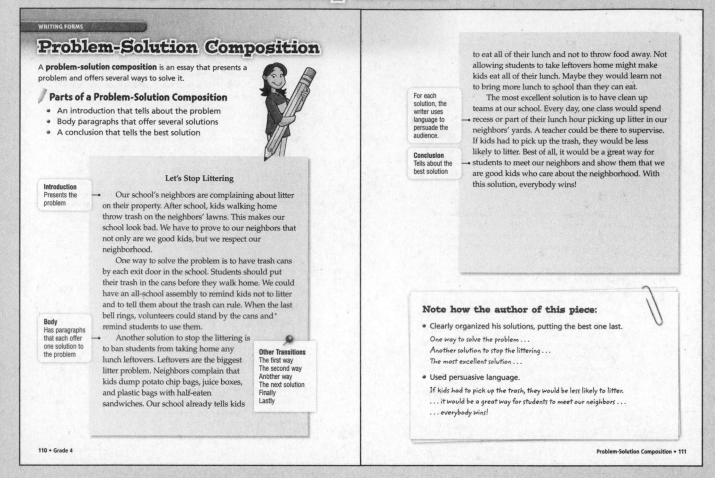

Problem-Solution Composition

A **problem-solution composition** is an essay that presents a problem and offers several ways to solve it.

Parts of a Problem-Solution Composition
- An introduction that tells about the problem
- Body paragraphs that offer several solutions
- A conclusion that tells the best solution

Introduction
Presents the problem

Let's Stop Littering

Our school's neighbors are complaining about litter on their property. After school, kids walking home throw trash on the neighbors' lawns. This makes our school look bad. We have to prove to our neighbors that not only are we good kids, but we respect our neighborhood.

One way to solve the problem is to have trash cans by each exit door in the school. Students should put their trash in the cans before they walk home. We could have an all-school assembly to remind kids not to litter and to tell them about the trash can rule. When the last bell rings, volunteers could stand by the cans and remind students to use them.

Body
Has paragraphs that each offer one solution to the problem

Another solution to stop the littering is to ban students from taking home any lunch leftovers. Leftovers are the biggest litter problem. Neighbors complain that kids dump potato chip bags, juice boxes, and plastic bags with half-eaten sandwiches. Our school already tells kids

Other Transitions
The first way
The second way
Another way
The next solution
Finally
Lastly

110 • Grade 4

to eat all of their lunch and not to throw food away. Not allowing students to take leftovers home might make kids eat all of their lunch. Maybe they would learn not to bring more lunch to school than they can eat.

For each solution, the writer uses language to persuade the audience.

The most excellent solution is to have clean up teams at our school. Every day, one class would spend recess or part of their lunch hour picking up litter in our neighbors' yards. A teacher could be there to supervise. If kids had to pick up the trash, they would be less likely to litter. Best of all, it would be a great way for students to meet our neighbors and show them that we are good kids who care about the neighborhood. With this solution, everybody wins!

Conclusion
Tells about the best solution

Note how the author of this piece:
- Clearly organized his solutions, putting the best one last.
  One way to solve the problem . . .
  Another solution to stop the littering . . .
  The most excellent solution . . .
- Used persuasive language.
  If kids had to pick up the trash, they would be less likely to litter.
  . . . it would be a great way for students to meet our neighbors . . .
  . . . everybody wins!

Problem-Solution Composition • 111

Minilesson 97

Understanding Problem and Solution

Objective: Understand the problem/solution composition.

Guiding Question: How do I use these pages to help me write a good problem/solution composition?

Teach/Model

Ask students to read the definition and bulleted points. Tell them that the example on these pages presents solutions to the problem of students' littering near the school. Then have students read to the end of p. 111.

Practice/Apply

Have students identify the three solutions that the author presented in this essay.

Minilesson 98

Using Order of Importance

Objective: Organize solutions in order of importance.

Guiding Question: How will I organize my solutions in a problem/solution composition?

Teach/Model

Point out how the author organized the solutions in this essay. Explain that he put the best solution last. Elicit that the author did this to make a strong argument that will convince his audience.

Practice/Apply

Have students brainstorm three solutions to a problem in your school, such as bullying or switching to healthy snacks. Have students list their solutions in order of importance, with the best solution last.

Compare-and-Contrast Essay

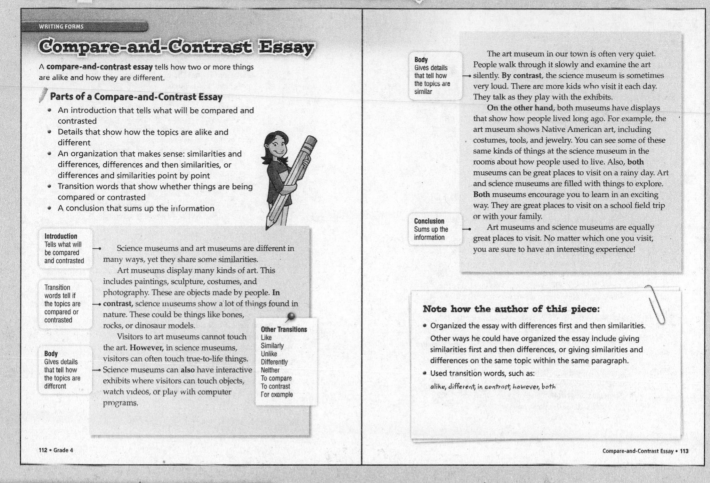

Minilesson 99

Understanding the Compare-and-Contrast Essay

Objective: Understand the compare-and-contrast essay.

Guiding Question: How can I use these pages to help me write a good compare-and-contrast essay?

Teach/Model

Have students read the definition and bulleted points. Explain that the essay on these pages compares and contrasts science museums and art museums. Then have students read to the end of p. 113.

Practice/Apply

Have students create a Venn diagram. Direct them to fill in the diagram with details from the essay that tell how science and art museums are alike and different.

Minilesson 100

Using Transitions to Signal Comparisons and Contrasts

Objective: Use transitions to signal comparisons and contrasts.

Guiding Question: How do I use transition words to make my compare-and-contrast essay clear?

Teach/Model

Point out boldfaced words in this essay, such as *in contrast, however, also,* and *both.* Explain to students that the author used transition words to signal comparisons and contrasts.

Practice/Apply

Have students discuss how transition words help them understand the topic and the organization of the essay.

How-to Essay

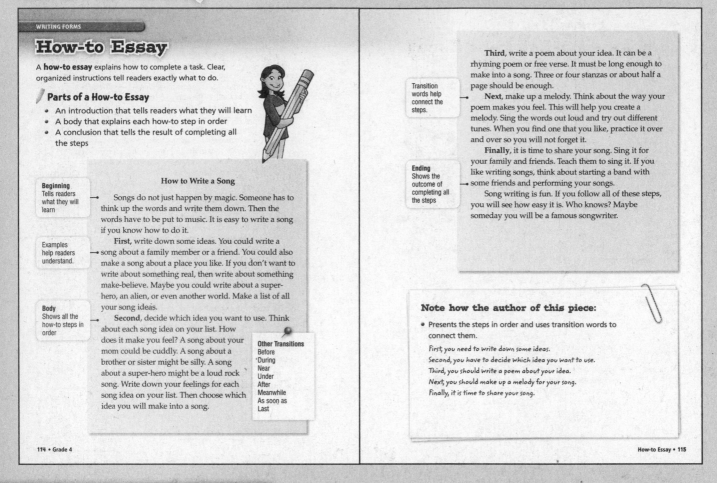

Minilesson 101

Understanding the How-to Essay

Objective: Understand how to use the information presented about the how-to essay.

Guiding Question: How can I use these pages to help me write a good how-to essay?

Teach/Model

Have students read the definition and bulleted points. Add that a how-to essay should mention any materials required to complete the task. Have the students read to the end of p. 115. Point out that the boldfaced transition words show how the steps connect in order.

Practice/Apply

Have students locate and tell how the introduction and conclusion do what the bulleted points say they will do.

Minilesson 102

Using Sequential Order

Objective: Put steps in order.

Guiding Question: How do I connect my steps in a how-to essay without numbering them?

Teach/Model

Explain to students that the writer linked ideas in this essay with sequence words such as *first, second,* and *finally,* which replace numbered steps in a how-to essay.

Practice/Apply

Have students locate the boldface transition words and discuss other sequence words that might be used in place of them. (Examples: *after this* or *then* for *next; last* instead of *finally.*)

Explanation

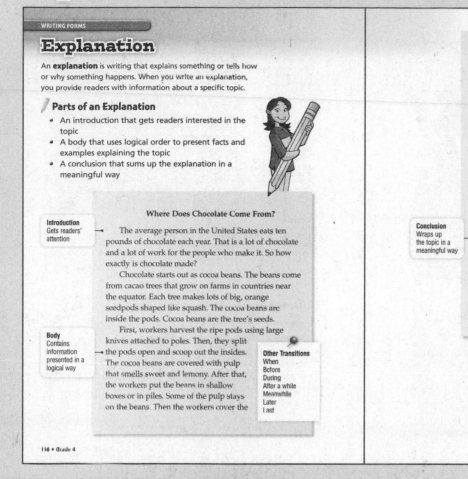

WRITING FORMS

Explanation

An **explanation** is writing that explains something or tells how or why something happens. When you write an explanation, you provide readers with information about a specific topic.

Parts of an Explanation

- An introduction that gets readers interested in the topic
- A body that uses logical order to present facts and examples explaining the topic
- A conclusion that sums up the explanation in a meaningful way

Where Does Chocolate Come From?

Introduction
Gets readers' attention

The average person in the United States eats ten pounds of chocolate each year. That is a lot of chocolate and a lot of work for the people who make it. So how exactly is chocolate made?

Chocolate starts out as cocoa beans. The beans come from cacao trees that grow on farms in countries near the equator. Each tree makes lots of big, orange seedpods shaped like squash. The cocoa beans are inside the pods. Cocoa beans are the tree's seeds.

Body
Contains information presented in a logical way

First, workers harvest the ripe pods using large knives attached to poles. Then, they split the pods open and scoop out the insides. The cocoa beans are covered with pulp that smells sweet and lemony. After that, the workers put the beans in shallow boxes or in piles. Some of the pulp stays on the beans. Then the workers cover the

Other Transitions
When
Before
During
After a while
Meanwhile
Later
Last

beans with big banana leaves. After about a week in the sun, the pulp breaks down and the beans begin to taste like chocolate. Next, the workers put the beans on bamboo mats to dry. The beans are dried for several days. During this drying process, the beans lose most of their moisture and about half their weight. The dried beans are hard. They have a deep brown center, and they smell like chocolate. Now the workers load the cocoa beans into sacks. They put the sacks onto trucks, boats, and planes and send them to chocolate factories all around the world.

Finally, chocolate makers in the factories roast the beans and grind them up. The ground cocoa beans turn into a thick chocolate liquid. The liquid is made into solid unsweetened chocolate, cocoa butter, or cocoa powder. Other ingredients can be added to sweeten and flavor the chocolate.

Conclusion
Wraps up the topic in a meaningful way

It takes a lot of work to make cocoa beans into chocolate. But once you have chocolate, you can use it to make other things. Most of them are sweet, like cakes, candy, ice cream, and cookies. Unsweetened chocolate can also be mixed with spicy ingredients like onions, garlic, and chili peppers to make a special sauce for Mexican meals. However you use it, chocolate is one of the most delicious foods you will ever eat.

116 • Grade 4

Explanation • 117

WRITING MODELS AND FORMS

Minilesson 103

Understanding the Explanation

Objective: Understand the explanation.

Guiding Question: How can I use these pages to help me write a good explanation?

Teach/Model

Have students read the definition and bulleted points. Point out that the example on these pages explains where chocolate comes from. Then have students read to the end of p. 117.

Practice/Apply

Write this question on the board: *Where does chocolate come from?* Have students give an answer based on their reading of this explanation.

Minilesson 104

Using Precise Words and Phrases

Objective: Use precise words and phrases.

Guiding Question: What precise words and phrases can I use to make my explanation clear?

Teach/Model

Point out examples of precise words and phrases in the fourth paragraph: *roast, ground cocoa beans, thick chocolate liquid.* Mention that the author used precise language to make this explanation clear.

Practice/Apply

On the board, write *Chocolate comes in different ways.* Have students rewrite the sentence with precise words and phrases. (Example: *Chocolate comes in different forms such as bars, chips, and chunks.*)

Science Observation Report

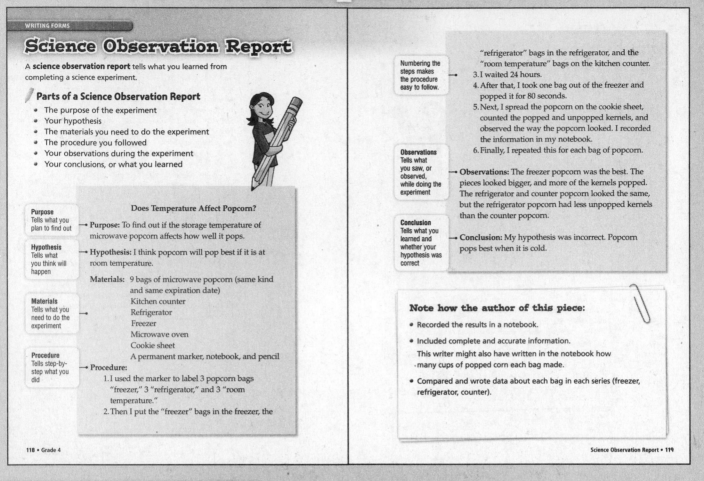

Minilesson 105

Understanding the Science Observation Report

Objective: Understand the science observation report.

Guiding Question: How can I use these pages to help me write a good science observation report?

Teach/Model

Tell students to read the definition and bulleted points. Explain that the example on these pages is a science observation report about a microwave popcorn experiment. Have students read to the end of p. 119.

Practice/Apply

Have students discuss the purpose, hypothesis, and conclusion of this microwave popcorn experiment.

Minilesson 106

Using Time-Order Words

Objective: Use time-order words to explain a procedure.

Guiding Question: How can I use time-order words to make my science observation report clear?

Teach/Model

Explain to students that the author used time-order words to explain the step-by-step procedure in this report. Point out that time-order words such as *Then* and *After that* help make the order of the steps clear.

Practice/Apply

Have students identify other time-order words in this report. (Examples: *Next, Finally*) Have them discuss how using time-order words and numbering the steps makes the procedure easy to follow.

Research Report

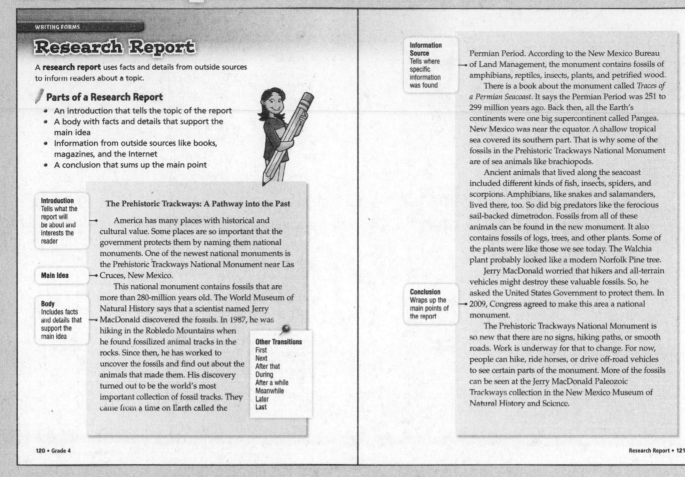

WRITING FORMS

Research Report

A **research report** uses facts and details from outside sources to inform readers about a topic.

Parts of a Research Report

- An introduction that tells the topic of the report
- A body with facts and details that support the main idea
- Information from outside sources like books, magazines, and the Internet
- A conclusion that sums up the main point

Introduction
Tells what the report will be about and interests the reader

Main Idea

Body
Includes facts and details that support the main idea

The Prehistoric Trackways: A Pathway into the Past

America has many places with historical and cultural value. Some places are so important that the government protects them by naming them national monuments. One of the newest national monuments is the Prehistoric Trackways National Monument near Las Cruces, New Mexico.

This national monument contains fossils that are more than 280-million years old. The World Museum of Natural History says that a scientist named Jerry MacDonald discovered the fossils. In 1987, he was hiking in the Robledo Mountains when he found fossilized animal tracks in the rocks. Since then, he has worked to uncover the fossils and find out about the animals that made them. His discovery turned out to be the world's most important collection of fossil tracks. They came from a time on Earth called the

Other Transitions
First
Next
After that
During
After a while
Meanwhile
Later
Last

120 • Grade 4

Information Source
Tells where specific information was found

Permian Period. According to the New Mexico Bureau of Land Management, the monument contains fossils of amphibians, reptiles, insects, plants, and petrified wood.

There is a book about the monument called *Traces of a Permian Seacoast*. It says the Permian Period was 251 to 299 million years ago. Back then, all the Earth's continents were one big supercontinent called Pangea. New Mexico was near the equator. A shallow tropical sea covered its southern part. That is why some of the fossils in the Prehistoric Trackways National Monument are of sea animals like brachiopods.

Ancient animals that lived along the seacoast included different kinds of fish, insects, spiders, and scorpions. Amphibians, like snakes and salamanders, lived there, too. So did big predators like the ferocious sail-backed dimetrodon. Fossils from all of these animals can be found in the new monument. It also contains fossils of logs, trees, and other plants. Some of the plants were like those we see today. The Walchia plant probably looked like a modern Norfolk Pine tree.

Jerry MacDonald worried that hikers and all-terrain vehicles might destroy these valuable fossils. So, he asked the United States Government to protect them. In 2009, Congress agreed to make this area a national monument.

Conclusion
Wraps up the main points of the report

The Prehistoric Trackways National Monument is so new that there are no signs, hiking paths, or smooth roads. Work is underway for that to change. For now, people can hike, ride horses, or drive off-road vehicles to see certain parts of the monument. More of the fossils can be seen at the Jerry MacDonald Paleozoic Trackways collection in the New Mexico Museum of Natural History and Science.

Research Report • 121

WRITING MODELS AND FORMS

Minilesson 107

Understanding the Research Report

Objective: Understand the research report.

Guiding Question: How can I use these pages to help me write a good research report?

Teach/Model

Ask students to read the definition and bulleted points. Explain that the example on these pages is a report about Prehistoric Trackways National Monument. Add that research reports give information in the author's own words and often include a works-cited page at the end. Then have students read to the end of p. 121.

Practice/Apply

Have students identify the main idea of this research report and three facts and details that support it.

Minilesson 108

Identifying Sources of Information

Objective: Identify outside sources of information.

Guiding Question: How do I tell where I found information for my report?

Teach/Model

Explain to students that one way to identify a source of information is by citing it in the report itself. Discuss how the author did this in the second paragraph. Point out the sentence that begins *According to the New Mexico Bureau of Land Management.*

Practice/Apply

Have students find two other information sources the author cites in this report. *(World Museum of Natural History, Traces of a Permian Seacoast)*

Graphs, Diagrams, and Charts

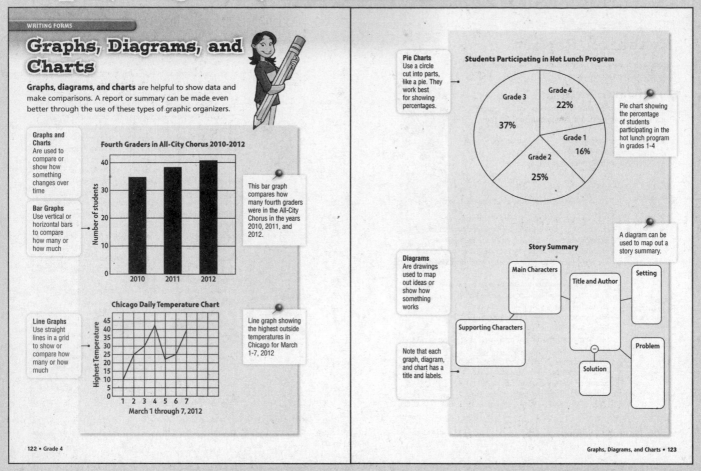

Graphs, Diagrams, and Charts

Graphs, diagrams, and charts are helpful to show data and make comparisons. A report or summary can be made even better through the use of these types of graphic organizers.

Graphs and Charts
Are used to compare or show how something changes over time

Fourth Graders in All-City Chorus 2010-2012

This bar graph compares how many fourth graders were in the All-City Chorus in the years 2010, 2011, and 2012.

Bar Graphs
Use vertical or horizontal bars to compare how many or how much

Line Graphs
Use straight lines in a grid to show or compare how many or how much

Chicago Daily Temperature Chart

Line graph showing the highest outside temperatures in Chicago for March 1-7, 2012

Pie Charts
Use a circle cut into parts, like a pie. They work best for showing percentages.

Students Participating in Hot Lunch Program

- Grade 3 — 37%
- Grade 4 — 22%
- Grade 1 — 16%
- Grade 2 — 25%

Pie chart showing the percentage of students participating in the hot lunch program in grades 1-4

Diagrams
Are drawings used to map out ideas or show how something works

Note that each graph, diagram, and chart has a title and labels.

Story Summary

A diagram can be used to map out a story summary.

- Main Characters
- Supporting Characters
- Title and Author
- Setting
- Problem
- Solution

Minilesson 109

Understanding Graphs, Diagrams, and Charts

Objective: Understand graphs, diagrams, and charts.

Guiding Question: How do I use graphs, diagrams, or charts to make my report or summary better?

Teach/Model

Have students read the definition on p. 122. Then discuss each of the examples given on these pages.

Practice/Apply

Have students use the first three graphic organizers to answer these questions: *In which year were the most fourth graders in All-City Chorus? Which March day was warmest in Chicago? Which grade has 37 percent of its students in the hot lunch program?*

Minilesson 110

Using Titles and Labels

Objective: Use titles and labels on graphic organizers.

Guiding Question: What titles and labels can I use to make my graphs, diagrams, and charts clear?

Teach/Model

Explain to students that using titles and labels on graphic organizers helps the reader interpret the information that is shown. Point out that the bar graph, line graph, pie chart, and story summary on these pages all have clear titles and labels.

Practice/Apply

Have students create a bar graph, a line graph, or a pie chart to represent data about their classroom or school. Remind them to use a clear title and labels.

Character Description

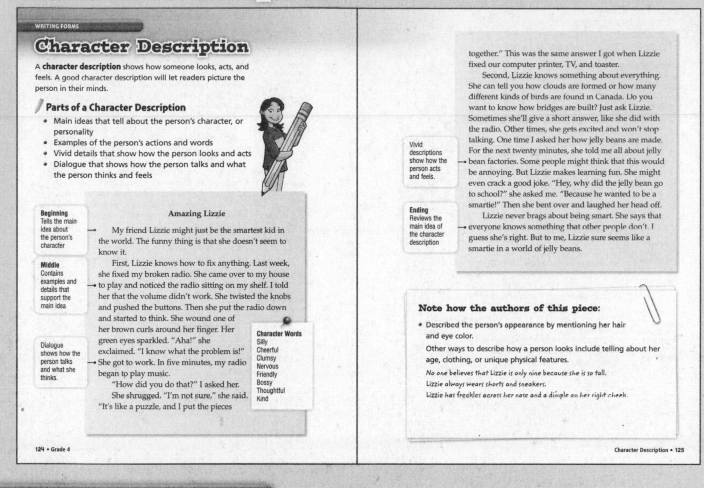

Minilesson 111

Understanding the Character Description

Objective: Understand character description.

Guiding Question: How do I use these pages to help me write a good character description?

Teach/Model

Ask students to read the definition and the bulleted points. Explain that the example on these pages describes a character named Lizzie. Point out that the author described how Lizzie looks, acts, and feels. Then have students read to the end of p. 125.

Practice/Apply

Have students write a short scene describing something else Lizzie might do based on the details provided in the character description. Encourage them to draw a picture of her.

Minilesson 112

Using Vivid Details

Objective: Use vivid details to bring a character to life.

Guiding Question: What details will I use to describe how a character looks, acts, and feels?

Teach/Model

Explain that the author used vivid details to describe Lizzie. Point out these details: *She wound one of her brown curls around her finger* and *she bent over and laughed her head off.* Tell students that these details help the reader picture what Lizzie looks like and how she acts.

Practice/Apply

Have students write sentences describing a real person or an imaginary character. Ask them to add at least three vivid details.

Personal Narrative

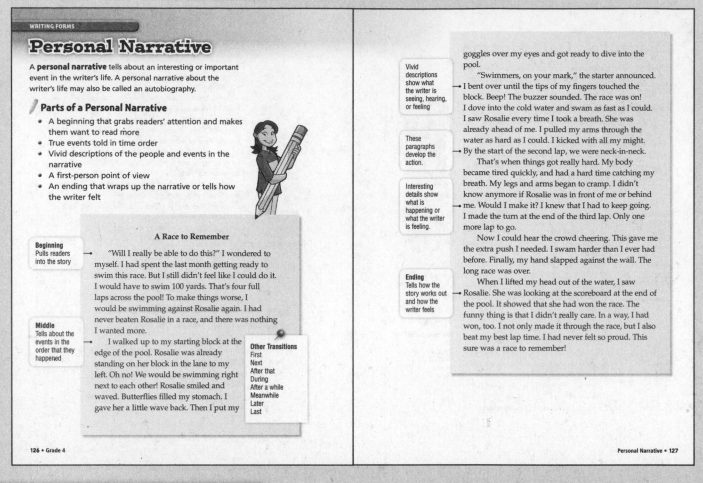

WRITING FORMS

Personal Narrative

A **personal narrative** tells about an interesting or important event in the writer's life. A personal narrative about the writer's life may also be called an autobiography.

Parts of a Personal Narrative

- A beginning that grabs readers' attention and makes them want to read more
- True events told in time order
- Vivid descriptions of the people and events in the narrative
- A first-person point of view
- An ending that wraps up the narrative or tells how the writer felt

A Race to Remember

Beginning
Pulls readers into the story

"Will I really be able to do this?" I wondered to myself. I had spent the last month getting ready to swim this race. But I still didn't feel like I could do it. I would have to swim 100 yards. That's four full laps across the pool! To make things worse, I would be swimming against Rosalie again. I had never beaten Rosalie in a race, and there was nothing I wanted more.

Middle
Tells about the events in the order that they happened

I walked up to my starting block at the edge of the pool. Rosalie was already standing on her block in the lane to my left. Oh no! We would be swimming right next to each other! Rosalie smiled and waved. Butterflies filled my stomach. I gave her a little wave back. Then I put my

Other Transitions
First
Next
After that
During
After a while
Meanwhile
Later
Last

126 • Grade 4

Vivid descriptions show what the writer is seeing, hearing, or feeling

These paragraphs develop the action.

Interesting details show what is happening or what the writer is feeling.

Ending Tells how the story works out and how the writer feels

goggles over my eyes and got ready to dive into the pool.

"Swimmers, on your mark," the starter announced. I bent over until the tips of my fingers touched the block. Beep! The buzzer sounded. The race was on! I dove into the cold water and swam as fast as I could. I saw Rosalie every time I took a breath. She was already ahead of me. I pulled my arms through the water as hard as I could. I kicked with all my might. By the start of the second lap, we were neck-in-neck.

That's when things got really hard. My body became tired quickly, and had a hard time catching my breath. My legs and arms began to cramp. I didn't know anymore if Rosalie was in front of me or behind me. Would I make it? I knew that I had to keep going. I made the turn at the end of the third lap. Only one more lap to go.

Now I could hear the crowd cheering. This gave me the extra push I needed. I swam harder than I ever had before. Finally, my hand slapped against the wall. The long race was over.

When I lifted my head out of the water, I saw Rosalie. She was looking at the scoreboard at the end of the pool. It showed that she had won the race. The funny thing is that I didn't really care. In a way, I had won, too. I not only made it through the race, but I also beat my best lap time. I had never felt so proud. This sure was a race to remember!

Personal Narrative • 127

WRITING MODELS AND FORMS

Minilesson 113

Understanding the Personal Narrative

Objective: Understand the personal narrative.

Guiding Question: How can I use these pages to help me write a good personal narrative?

Teach/Model

Have students read the definition and bulleted points. Explain that the example on these pages is a personal narrative about a swimming race. Point out that the author used the first-person point of view: *I, me, my, myself.* Then ask students to read to the end of p. 127.

Practice/Apply

Have students list the interesting details and vivid descriptions in this personal narrative that help bring people and events to life.

Minilesson 114

Using Time Order

Objective: Tell events in the order in which they happened.

Guiding Question: How do I tell what happened in my personal narrative?

Teach/Model

Explain to students that a personal narrative tells what happened in time order. Point out that the author arranged events in the swimming race in the order in which they happened, linking them with transitions such as *Then* and *By the start of the second lap.*

Practice/Apply

Have students write about an important event in their own lives using time order to narrate the sequence of events.

Biography

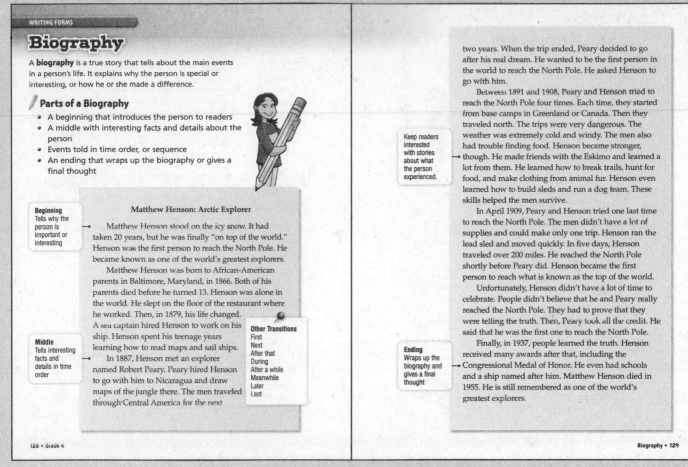

WRITING FORMS

Biography

A **biography** is a true story that tells about the main events in a person's life. It explains why the person is special or interesting, or how he or she made a difference.

Parts of a Biography

- A beginning that introduces the person to readers
- A middle with interesting facts and details about the person
- Events told in time order, or sequence
- An ending that wraps up the biography or gives a final thought

Matthew Henson: Arctic Explorer

Beginning
Tells why the person is important or interesting

    Matthew Henson stood on the icy snow. It had taken 20 years, but he was finally "on top of the world." Henson was the first person to reach the North Pole. He became known as one of the world's greatest explorers.

    Matthew Henson was born to African-American parents in Baltimore, Maryland, in 1866. Both of his parents died before he turned 13. Henson was alone in the world. He slept on the floor of the restaurant where he worked. Then, in 1879, his life changed. A sea captain hired Henson to work on his ship. Henson spent his teenage years learning how to read maps and sail ships.

Middle
Tells interesting facts and details in time order

    In 1887, Henson met an explorer named Robert Peary. Peary hired Henson to go with him to Nicaragua and draw maps of the jungle there. The men traveled through Central America for the next

Other Transitions
First
Next
After that
During
After a while
Meanwhile
Later
Last

two years. When the trip ended, Peary decided to go after his real dream. He wanted to be the first person in the world to reach the North Pole. He asked Henson to go with him.

    Between 1891 and 1908, Peary and Henson tried to reach the North Pole four times. Each time, they started from base camps in Greenland or Canada. Then they traveled north. The trips were very dangerous. The weather was extremely cold and windy. The men also had trouble finding food. Henson became stronger,

Keep readers interested with stories about what the person experienced.

though. He made friends with the Eskimo and learned a lot from them. He learned how to break trails, hunt for food, and make clothing from animal fur. Henson even learned how to build sleds and run a dog team. These skills helped the men survive.

    In April 1909, Peary and Henson tried one last time to reach the North Pole. The men didn't have a lot of supplies and could make only one trip. Henson ran the lead sled and moved quickly. In five days, Henson traveled over 200 miles. He reached the North Pole shortly before Peary did. Henson became the first person to reach what is known as the top of the world.

    Unfortunately, Henson didn't have a lot of time to celebrate. People didn't believe that he and Peary really reached the North Pole. They had to prove that they were telling the truth. Then, Peary took all the credit. He said that he was the first one to reach the North Pole.

Ending
Wraps up the biography and gives a final thought

    Finally, in 1937, people learned the truth. Henson received many awards after that, including the Congressional Medal of Honor. He even had schools and a ship named after him. Matthew Henson died in 1955. He is still remembered as one of the world's greatest explorers.

WRITING MODELS AND FORMS

Minilesson 115

Understanding the Biography

Objective: Understand the biography.

Guiding Question: How can I use these pages to help me write a good biography?

Teach/Model

Tell students to read the definition and the bulleted points on p. 128. Explain that the example on these pages is a biography of the African-American explorer Matthew Henson. Then have students read to the end of p. 129.

Practice/Apply

Have students discuss why Matthew Henson is important or how he made a difference based on their reading of facts and details in this biography.

Minilesson 116

Including Facts

Objective: Use facts to tell about a person's life.

Guiding Question: How do I include facts in my biography?

Teach/Model

Remind students that a biography includes details about a person's life. Explain that the author told about the main events in Matthew Henson's life, beginning with his birth and ending with his death. Point out that the author included facts like dates to describe when these happened. Point out the dates in the model.

Practice/Apply

Using dates and details in this biography, have students make a timeline of Matthew Henson's life.

Fictional Narrative

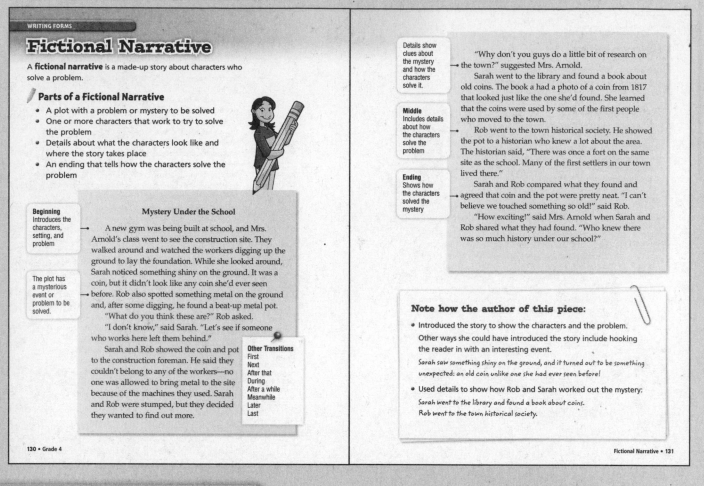

Minilesson 117

Understanding the Fictional Narrative

Objective: Understand the fictional narrative.

Guiding Question: How can I use these pages to help me write a good fictional narrative?

Teach/Model

Tell students to read the definition and bulleted points. Add that a fictional narrative includes dialogue. Have students read to the end of p. 131.

Practice/Apply

Have students list the details and dialogue that help them understand the characters and setting in this fictional narrative. Discuss how each detail contributes to the story.

Minilesson 118

Understanding Plot

Objective: Understand the plot of a fictional narrative.

Guiding Question: What elements do I include in the plot of my fictional narrative?

Teach/Model

Explain to students that the plot of a fictional narrative is the sequence of story events. It includes a problem the characters solve and a solution. Point out that the problem in "Mystery Under the School" is introduced in the beginning and solved in the middle and ending.

Practice/Apply

Have students list the sequence of story events in "Mystery Under the School." Make sure that they can identify the problem and how Rob and Sarah solve it.

Play

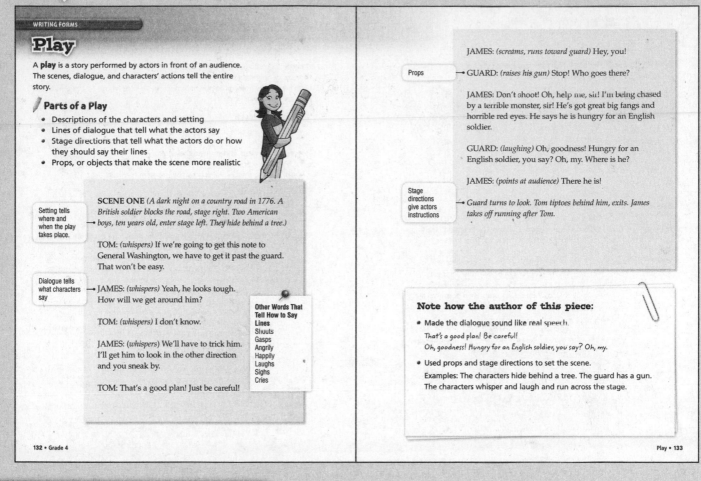

Play

A **play** is a story performed by actors in front of an audience. The scenes, dialogue, and characters' actions tell the entire story.

Parts of a Play

- Descriptions of the characters and setting
- Lines of dialogue that tell what the actors say
- Stage directions that tell what the actors do or how they should say their lines
- Props, or objects that make the scene more realistic

> Setting tells where and when the play takes place.

SCENE ONE (*A dark night on a country road in 1776. A British soldier blocks the road, stage right. Two American boys, ten years old, enter stage left. They hide behind a tree.*)

TOM: (*whispers*) If we're going to get this note to General Washington, we have to get it past the guard. That won't be easy.

> Dialogue tells what characters say

JAMES: (*whispers*) Yeah, he looks tough. How will we get around him?

TOM: (*whispers*) I don't know.

JAMES: (*whispers*) We'll have to trick him. I'll get him to look in the other direction and you sneak by.

TOM: That's a good plan! Just be careful!

> **Other Words That Tell How to Say Lines**
> Shouts
> Gasps
> Angrily
> Happily
> Laughs
> Sighs
> Cries

> Props

JAMES: (*screams, runs toward guard*) Hey, you!

GUARD: (*raises his gun*) Stop! Who goes there?

JAMES: Don't shoot! Oh, help me, sir! I'm being chased by a terrible monster, sir! He's got great big fangs and horrible red eyes. He says he is hungry for an English soldier.

GUARD: (*laughing*) Oh, goodness! Hungry for an English soldier, you say? Oh, my. Where is he?

JAMES: (*points at audience*) There he is!

> Stage directions give actors instructions

Guard turns to look. Tom tiptoes behind him, exits. James takes off running after Tom.

Note how the author of this piece:

- Made the dialogue sound like real speech.
  That's a good plan! Be careful!
  Oh, goodness! Hungry for an English soldier, you say? Oh, my.
- Used props and stage directions to set the scene.
  Examples: The characters hide behind a tree. The guard has a gun. The characters whisper and laugh and run across the stage.

132 • Grade 4

Play • 133

Minilesson 119

Understanding the Play

Objective: Understand the elements of a play.

Guiding Question: How can I use these pages to help me write a good play?

Teach/Model

Have students read the definition and bulleted points. Add that some plays are divided into acts and scenes. Explain that this scene from a play is set during the American Revolution in the 18th century. Then have students read to the end of p. 133.

Practice/Apply

Have students discuss how the setting, stage directions, and props help set this scene.

Minilesson 120

Using Dialogue

Objective: Use dialogue in a play.

Guiding Question: How do I use dialogue in a play?

Teach/Model

Explain to students that this play scene consists of lines of dialogue that are spoken by three actors who play Tom, James, and a British soldier. Point out that the characters' names are written in capital letters and the stage directions are written in italics.

Practice/Apply

Have three volunteers perform the play, reading lines of dialogue. Remind them to use the stage directions as a guide for how they should speak their lines. Next, ask students to write dialogue for the following scene in the play.

Writing • **103**

Tall Tale/Myth

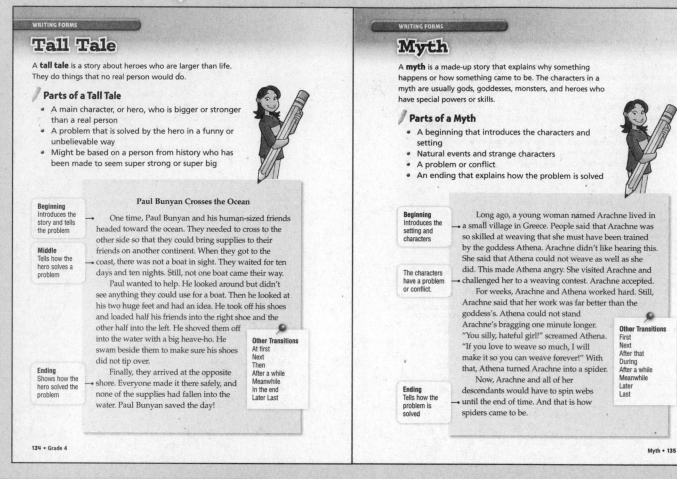

Tall Tale

A **tall tale** is a story about heroes who are larger than life. They do things that no real person would do.

Parts of a Tall Tale

- A main character, or hero, who is bigger or stronger than a real person
- A problem that is solved by the hero in a funny or unbelievable way
- Might be based on a person from history who has been made to seem super strong or super big

Paul Bunyan Crosses the Ocean

Beginning
Introduces the story and tells the problem

One time, Paul Bunyan and his human-sized friends headed toward the ocean. They needed to cross to the other side so that they could bring supplies to their friends on another continent. When they got to the coast, there was not a boat in sight. They waited for ten days and ten nights. Still, not one boat came their way.

Middle
Tells how the hero solves a problem

Paul wanted to help. He looked around but didn't see anything they could use for a boat. Then he looked at his two huge feet and had an idea. He took off his shoes and loaded half his friends into the right shoe and the other half into the left. He shoved them off into the water with a big heave-ho. He swam beside them to make sure his shoes did not tip over.

Ending
Shows how the hero solved the problem

Finally, they arrived at the opposite shore. Everyone made it there safely, and none of the supplies had fallen into the water. Paul Bunyan saved the day!

Other Transitions
At first
Next
Then
After a while
Meanwhile
In the end
Later Last

134 • Grade 4

Myth

A **myth** is a made-up story that explains why something happens or how something came to be. The characters in a myth are usually gods, goddesses, monsters, and heroes who have special powers or skills.

Parts of a Myth

- A beginning that introduces the characters and setting
- Natural events and strange characters
- A problem or conflict
- An ending that explains how the problem is solved

Beginning
Introduces the setting and characters

Long ago, a young woman named Arachne lived in a small village in Greece. People said that Arachne was so skilled at weaving that she must have been trained by the goddess Athena. Arachne didn't like hearing this. She said that Athena could not weave as well as she did. This made Athena angry. She visited Arachne and challenged her to a weaving contest. Arachne accepted.

The characters have a problem or conflict.

For weeks, Arachne and Athena worked hard. Still, Arachne said that her work was far better than the goddess's. Athena could not stand Arachne's bragging one minute longer. "You silly, hateful girl!" screamed Athena. "If you love to weave so much, I will make it so you can weave forever!" With that, Athena turned Arachne into a spider.

Ending
Tells how the problem is solved

Now, Arachne and all of her descendants would have to spin webs until the end of time. And that is how spiders came to be.

Other Transitions
First
Next
After that
During
After a while
Meanwhile
Later
Last

Myth • 135

WRITING MODELS AND FORMS

Minilesson 121

Understanding the Tall Tale

Objective: Understand the tall tale.

Guiding Question: How can I use this page to help me write a tall tale?

Teach/Model

Ask students to read the definition and the bulleted points on p. 134. Explain that the tall tale on this page, "Paul Bunyan Crosses the Ocean," is about a hero who solves a problem in an unbelievable way. Then have students read to the end of the page.

Practice/Apply

Have students discuss the characteristics that make Paul Bunyan a hero. Encourage them to recall stories about other heroes they have read about in tall tales and write their own brief tall tale.

Minilesson 122

Understanding the Myth

Objective: Understand the myth.

Guiding Question: How can I use this page to help me write a myth?

Teach/Model

Have students read the definition and bulleted points on p. 135. Explain that the example on this page is a retelling of a Greek myth about a weaver named Arachne and the goddess Athena. Ask students to read to the end of the page.

Practice/Apply

Have students discuss the setting, the characters, and the conflict in this myth. Ask *According to this myth, how did spiders come to be?* Have students share other myths they have heard.

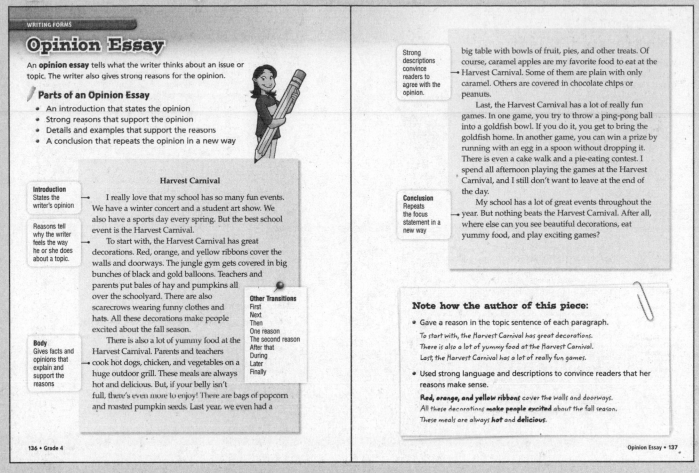

Minilesson 123

Understanding the Opinion Essay

Objective: Understand the opinion essay.

Guiding Question: How can I use these pages to help me write a good opinion essay?

Teach/Model

Tell students to read the definition and the bulleted points that follow it. Explain that the opinion essay on these pages tells what the author thinks about the school's yearly Harvest Carnival. Then have students read to the end of p. 137.

Practice/Apply

Have students look at the introduction and the conclusion of the essay. Have them write the author's opinion statement in their own words.

Minilesson 124

Supporting Opinions with Strong Reasons

Objective: Use strong reasons to support an opinion.

Guiding Question: What reasons will I use to support my opinion in an opinion essay?

Teach/Model

Explain to students that the author's opinion about the Harvest Carnival is supported with strong reasons. Point out transition words, such as *To start with* and *Last,* that link the opinion and reasons that support it.

Practice/Apply

Have students list three reasons from the essay that support the author's opinion. Then have them find details and examples that support each reason.

Persuasive Essay

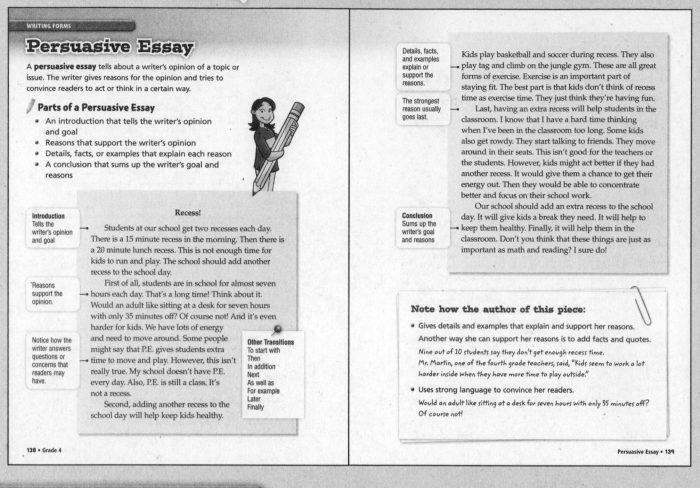

WRITING FORMS

Persuasive Essay

A **persuasive essay** tells about a writer's opinion of a topic or issue. The writer gives reasons for the opinion and tries to convince readers to act or think in a certain way.

Parts of a Persuasive Essay
- An introduction that tells the writer's opinion and goal
- Reasons that support the writer's opinion
- Details, facts, or examples that explain each reason
- A conclusion that sums up the writer's goal and reasons

Introduction
Tells the writer's opinion and goal

Reasons support the opinion.

Notice how the writer answers questions or concerns that readers may have.

Recess!

Students at our school get two recesses each day. There is a 15 minute recess in the morning. Then there is a 20 minute lunch recess. This is not enough time for kids to run and play. The school should add another recess to the school day.

First of all, students are in school for almost seven hours each day. That's a long time! Think about it. Would an adult like sitting at a desk for seven hours with only 35 minutes off? Of course not! And it's even harder for kids. We have lots of energy and need to move around. Some people might say that P.E. gives students extra time to move and play. However, this isn't really true. My school doesn't have P.E. every day. Also, P.E. is still a class. It's not a recess.

Second, adding another recess to the school day will help keep kids healthy.

Other Transitions
To start with
Then
In addition
Next
As well as
For example
Later
Finally

Details, facts, and examples explain or support the reasons.

The strongest reason usually goes last.

Kids play basketball and soccer during recess. They also play tag and climb on the jungle gym. These are all great forms of exercise. Exercise is an important part of staying fit. The best part is that kids don't think of recess time as exercise time. They just think they're having fun.

Last, having an extra recess will help students in the classroom. I know that I have a hard time thinking when I've been in the classroom too long. Some kids also get rowdy. They start talking to friends. They move around in their seats. This isn't good for the teachers or the students. However, kids might act better if they had another recess. It would give them a chance to get their energy out. Then they would be able to concentrate better and focus on their school work.

Conclusion
Sums up the writer's goal and reasons

Our school should add an extra recess to the school day. It will give kids a break they need. It will help to keep them healthy. Finally, it will help them in the classroom. Don't you think that these things are just as important as math and reading? I sure do!

Note how the author of this piece:
- Gives details and examples that explain and support her reasons. Another way she can support her reasons is to add facts and quotes.
  Nine out of 10 students say they don't get enough recess time.
  Mr. Martin, one of the fourth grade teachers, said, "Kids seem to work a lot harder inside when they have more time to play outside."
- Uses strong language to convince her readers.
  Would an adult like sitting at a desk for seven hours with only 35 minutes off? Of course not!

WRITING MODELS AND FORMS

Minilesson 125

Understanding the Persuasive Essay

Objective: Understand the persuasive essay.

Guiding Question: How can I use these pages to help me write a good persuasive essay?

Teach/Model

Ask students to read the definition and bulleted points. Explain that the persuasive essay on these pages tells about the author's opinion of recess at her school. Then have students read to the end of p. 139.

Practice/Apply

Have students look at the introduction and the conclusion of the essay. Ask them to explain the author's opinion about recess at her school and her goal.

Minilesson 126

Using Persuasive Language

Objective: Use strong language to convince an audience.

Guiding Question: What words and phrases can I use in my persuasive essay to convince my readers?

Teach/Model

Tell students that a persuasive essay uses strong, convincing words. Point out examples of persuasive language in this essay, such as *That's a long time!* and *I sure do!* Explain that the author used persuasive language to convince readers to accept her viewpoint.

Practice/Apply

Have students find other examples of strong words and phrases that the author used in this essay to convince her readers.

Response to Literature: Play

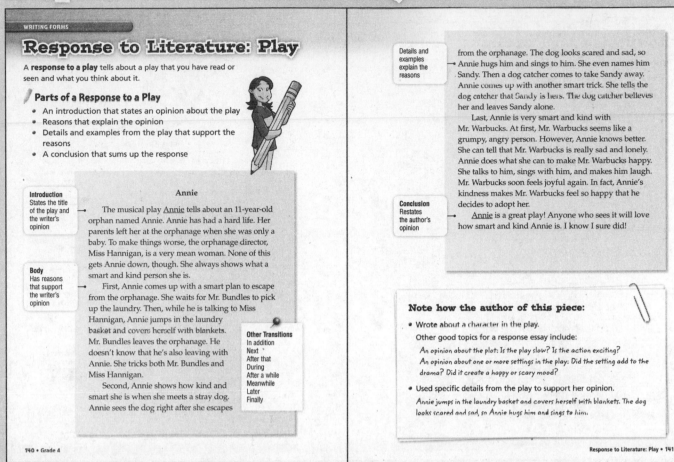

Response to Literature: Play

A **response to a play** tells about a play that you have read or seen and what you think about it.

Parts of a Response to a Play

- An introduction that states an opinion about the play
- Reasons that explain the opinion
- Details and examples from the play that support the reasons
- A conclusion that sums up the response

Introduction
States the title of the play and the writer's opinion

Body
Has reasons that support the writer's opinion

Annie

The musical play Annie tells about an 11-year-old orphan named Annie. Annie has had a hard life. Her parents left her at the orphanage when she was only a baby. To make things worse, the orphanage director, Miss Hannigan, is a very mean woman. None of this gets Annie down, though. She always shows what a smart and kind person she is.

First, Annie comes up with a smart plan to escape from the orphanage. She waits for Mr. Bundles to pick up the laundry. Then, while he is talking to Miss Hannigan, Annie jumps in the laundry basket and covers herself with blankets. Mr. Bundles leaves the orphanage. He doesn't know that he's also leaving with Annie. She tricks both Mr. Bundles and Miss Hannigan.

Second, Annie shows how kind and smart she is when she meets a stray dog. Annie sees the dog right after she escapes

Other Transitions
In addition
Next
After that
During
After a while
Meanwhile
Later
Finally

140 • Grade 4

Details and examples explain the reasons

from the orphanage. The dog looks scared and sad, so Annie hugs him and sings to him. She even names him Sandy. Then a dog catcher comes to take Sandy away. Annie comes up with another smart trick. She tells the dog catcher that Sandy is hers. The dog catcher believes her and leaves Sandy alone.

Last, Annie is very smart and kind with Mr. Warbucks. At first, Mr. Warbucks seems like a grumpy, angry person. However, Annie knows better. She can tell that Mr. Warbucks is really sad and lonely. Annie does what she can to make Mr. Warbucks happy. She talks to him, sings with him, and makes him laugh. Mr. Warbucks soon feels joyful again. In fact, Annie's kindness makes Mr. Warbucks feel so happy that he decides to adopt her.

Conclusion
Restates the author's opinion

Annie is a great play! Anyone who sees it will love how smart and kind Annie is. I know I sure did!

Note how the author of this piece:

- Wrote about a character in the play.

  Other good topics for a response essay include:

  An opinion about the plot: Is the play slow? Is the action exciting?

  An opinion about one or more settings in the play: Did the setting add to the drama? Did it create a happy or scary mood?

- Used specific details from the play to support her opinion.

  Annie jumps in the laundry basket and covers herself with blankets. The dog looks scared and sad, so Annie hugs him and sings to him.

Response to Literature: Play • 141

Minilesson 127

Understanding the Response to a Play

Objective: Understand a response essay about a play.

Guiding Question: How can I use these pages to help me write a good response to a play?

Teach/Model

Ask students to read the definition and the bulleted points that follow it. Explain that the response to a play on these pages tells how the author felt about the musical play *Annie*. Then instruct students to read to the end of p. 141.

Practice/Apply

Have students write an opinion about a play that they have read or seen. Challenge them to list reasons that explain their opinions.

Minilesson 128

Using Specific Details and Examples

Objective: Use strong details and examples as support.

Guiding Question: What details and examples should I use to explain the reasons in my response essay?

Teach/Model

Tell students that the author used strong details and examples from *Annie* to explain her opinion about the play. For example, the detail *She tricks both Mr. Bundles and Miss Hannigan* in the second paragraph supports the reason that Annie is smart.

Practice/Apply

Have students find other details and examples from the play that the author uses to explain the reasons for her opinion.

Writing • 107

Response to Poetry

Response to Poetry

A **response to poetry** explains a writer's reactions to a poem.

Parts of a Response to Poetry

- An introduction that states the writer's opinion
- Examples from the poem that explain the opinion
- A conclusion that sums up the ideas

Lights Along Main Street

I walked along an average street
And noticed all the lights
Placed above the cold concrete
To brighten dark fall nights.

The lights were not yet switched on.
(It was barely after three!)
So I stopped and gazed upon
Sights only I could see—

A rainy night, all things damp,
A sky with clouds and grey.
And overhead, the first bright lamp,
Lighting up my way.

In the distance, more and more,
Lanterns, lamps, and lights.
An evening at first dark and bored
Now is fully bright.

People strolling, busy crowds,
The smell of cinnamon treats,
Music from a theater, loud,
Light up my mind's Main Street.

Lights Along Main Street

Introduction Introduces the poem, setting, and meaning

The poem "Lights Along Main Street" tells the story of a person walking along a street. The person is walking during the day. She notices the streetlights, even though they aren't on. She imagines what the lights will look like when it is nighttime. The person walking has a great imagination. She pictures a whole scene that isn't there, filling the poem with vivid images and descriptions.

Details show clues about the poem's meaning.

At the start of the poem, the author is walking along a street. She says it is "an average street." The poem's title names the street Main Street. I think she uses the words "average" and "main" so the poem could take place anywhere. It's also important that she's walking on an average street because later on, her imagination makes the street special.

Then, the author says it's "barely after three." This means it is daytime, and the lights aren't on yet. She wants to know what they look like, so she imagines. She says, "So I stopped and gazed upon / Sights only I could see—." Only she can see these sights because she is imagining them. At this point, I was so curious! She

Other Transitions
First
Next
After that
During
After a while
Meanwhile
Later
Last

Minilesson 129

Understanding the Response to Poetry

Objective: Understand a response to poetry.

Guiding Question: How can I use these pages to help me write a good response to poetry?

Teach/Model

Ask students to read the definition, bulleted points, and poem on p. 142. Explain that the composition starting on p. 143 is a response to "Lights Along Main Street." Then have students read to the end of p. 145.

Practice/Apply

After reading the composition, ask students to identify how the author feels about "Lights Along Main Street." Have them find reasons that explain this opinion.

Minilesson 130

Quoting Poetry Correctly

Objective: Quote two or more lines of poetry correctly.

Guiding Question: How do I quote two or more lines of poetry in my response to poetry composition?

Teach/Model

Point out the pair of quoted lines from "Lights Along Main Street" in the third paragraph of this composition. Explain that the author put quotation marks around the lines and used a slash (/) with a space before and after it to show where one line ends and the next begins.

Practice/Apply

Have students quote two consecutive lines from "Lights Along Main Street" or another poem to complete this sentence: *My two favorite lines are _____.*

Response to Poetry

Body
Digs in further to find meaning in the poem

could have imagined anything. She could have imagined a busy street with people walking and having fun. Instead, she imagines something very dark.

Indeed, she sees, "A rainy night, all things damp / A sky with clouds and grey." The author pictures a dark evening with rain. "All things damp" means that it has been raining for a long time. When it rains for a while, everything gets a little wet. **Further**, the author sees "clouds and grey." This sounds like the kind of night when you don't even want to go outside because it is so wet and rainy.

Next, the author sees "the first bright lamp." Here, I picture this dark scene where everything is sad and quiet. Then, out of the dim street scene, a light! The lamp is so bright that it stands out against the darkness. She says it is "lighting up my way." Now, she can see in front of her. Instead of seeing just the grey sky, the author can see the street. At first, she just sees more and more light. This means the street looks brighter.

More details help to discuss the poem's meaning.

Finally, in the light, everything looks happy. She sees people walking and gathering in a store. She also smells cinnamon and hears music. These lines are so important because these are the first people, smells, and sounds in the poem. Before, when it was dark outside, the poem was dark and empty. Now, when the lights are on, the poem is filled with people and things to smell and hear.

The last line is: "Light up my mind's Main Street." I like that the author says it is her mind's street, and not just any street. This is not "an average street" or even "Main Street" anymore. This shows that the author now loves the street. It is no longer dark and dreary outside. Now it is bright and full of music. All of this is in her imagination, so I think she is really happy.

Conclusion
Sums up the main idea of the poem

When I finished reading the poem, I looked back at the title: "Lights Along Main Street." I noticed that the focus of the title isn't darkness or rain. The focus is on light. The author never gets to see the lights turn on. However, she imagines what it would look like. Her imagination is so bright and full. I believe this is what the poem is about—finding excitement and happiness in dark places.

Note how the author of this piece:

• Ends the response by going back to the beginning (the title). The author also could have ended the piece by talking about something general in the poem:

I notice that the ideas of light and dark come up again and again in the poem.

• Shows what the poem did not say, but could have:

She could have imagined a busy street with people walking and having fun.

WRITING MODELS AND FORMS

Minilesson 131

Analyzing Sensory Details

Objective: Analyze sensory details in a response to poetry.

Guiding Question: How do I analyze a poem's sensory details in my composition?

Teach/Model

Have students reread the last stanza of "Lights Along Main Street" (p. 142). Point out the writer's discussion of details from this stanza in the sixth and seventh paragraphs (pp. 144–145). Explain that the writer analyzed sensory details to find the poem's meaning.

Practice/Apply

Have students make a chart with the headings *Sight, Sound, Smell, Touch.* Have them list details in "Lights Along Main Street" that appeal to these senses.

Minilesson 132

Analyzing Figurative Language

Objective: Analyze figurative language in a poetry response.

Guiding Question: How do I analyze a poem's figurative language for my composition?

Teach/Model

Ask students to reread the last stanza of "Lights Along Main Street" (p. 142). Point out the writer's discussion of the stanza's last line in the seventh paragraph (p. 145) of the composition. Explain that the writer analyzed "my mind's Main Street" to find the poem's meaning.

Practice/Apply

Have students identify the type of figurative language "my mind's Main Street" is and determine whether they agree with the writer's analysis of it.

Author Response

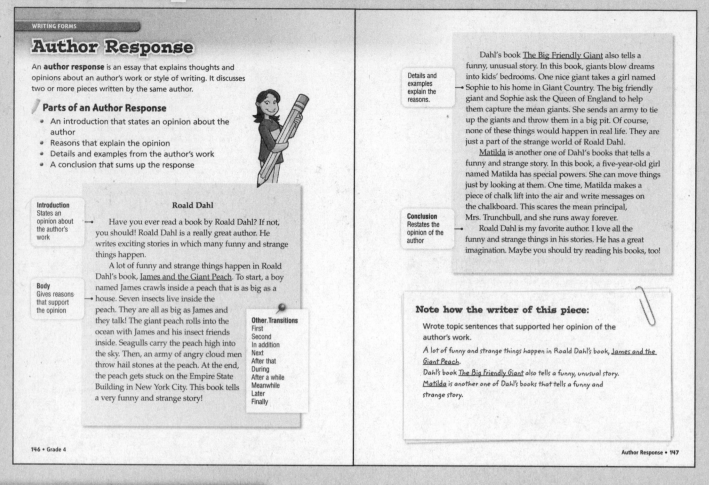

WRITING MODELS AND FORMS

Minilesson 133

Understanding the Author Response

Objective: Understand the author response essay.

Guiding Question: How can I use these pages to help me write a good author response?

Teach/Model

Ask students to read the definition and bulleted points. Tell them that the author response on these pages discusses three books by Roald Dahl. Then have students read to the end of p. 147.

Practice/Apply

Ask students to identify the opinion in this essay. Then have them find reasons that explain the opinion and details and examples that explain the reasons.

Minilesson 134

Writing Book Titles Correctly

Objective: Write book titles correctly.

Guiding Question: How do I write the titles of books in an author response essay?

Teach/Model

Call attention to the three books by Roald Dahl that are discussed in this author response essay. Tell students that book titles are underlined. Explain that the first, last, and important words are capitalized.

Practice/Apply

Have students think of an author they would like to write a response essay about. Have them list two books by this author, writing the titles correctly.

WRITING FORMS

Book Review/Report

A **book review or report** tells about a book that you've read. It gives a summary of the main ideas or events, the setting, and the characters.

Parts of a Book Report

- An introduction that tells basic information about the book, including its title, author, and main idea
- A body that tells about the most important parts of the book
- A conclusion that sums up the report

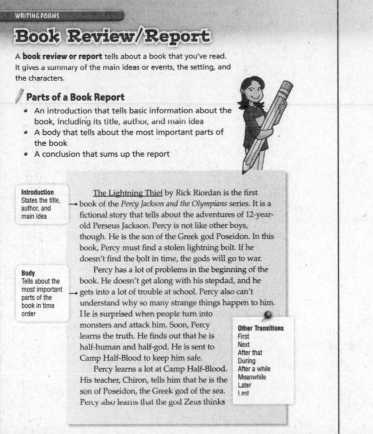

Introduction
States the title, author, and main idea

The Lightning Thief by Rick Riordan is the first book of the *Percy Jackson and the Olympians* series. It is a fictional story that tells about the adventures of 12-year-old Perseus Jackson. Percy is not like other boys, though. He is the son of the Greek god Poseidon. In this book, Percy must find a stolen lightning bolt. If he doesn't find the bolt in time, the gods will go to war.

Body
Tells about the most important parts of the book in time order

Percy has a lot of problems in the beginning of the book. He doesn't get along with his stepdad, and he gets into a lot of trouble at school. Percy also can't understand why so many strange things happen to him. He is surprised when people turn into monsters and attack him. Soon, Percy learns the truth. He finds out that he is half-human and half-god. He is sent to Camp Half-Blood to keep him safe.

Percy learns a lot at Camp Half-Blood. His teacher, Chiron, tells him that he is the son of Poseidon, the Greek god of the sea. Percy also learns that the god Zeus thinks

Other Transitions
First
Next
After that
During
After a while
Meanwhile
Later
Last

148 • Grade 4

These paragraphs give more information about the main characters and events.

that Poseidon stole his lightning bolt. If the bolt is not returned in 14 days, Zeus will go to war against Poseidon. Percy is given a quest. He must go to the Underworld, find the bolt, and return it to Zeus on Mount Olympus before the 14 days have passed. Percy takes two friends on the quest to help him. He takes Grover, a satyr, and Annabeth, the daughter of Athena.

Percy, Grover, and Annabeth must travel from New York to Los Angeles to get to the Underworld. The trip is hard. The friends battle monsters along the way. Ares, the god of war, plays a lot of tricks on them. Luckily, Percy has a special shield that keeps him safe.

Things don't get any easier for Percy when he finally gets to the Underworld. Hades, the god of the Underworld, says he doesn't have the bolt. Hades also says that his helm of darkness is missing. He accuses Percy of stealing both. To prove it, Hades says that the lightning bolt is in Percy's back pack. And it is! Percy, Grover, and Annabeth escape the Underworld and go back to New York.

At the end of the book, Percy goes to Mount Olympus on the 600th floor of the Empire State Building. He gives the lightning bolt to Zeus. He also meets his dad for the first time. Percy then tells the gods that he thinks the god Kronos caused all of the trouble. Kronos ruled before Zeus did. Now he wants to bring down the Greek gods. Percy leaves Mount Olympus at the end of the meeting. Everyone kneels and calls him a hero. Finally, Percy goes home to be with his mother.

Conclusion
Restates the title and author, and gives an opinion of the book

The Lightning Thief by Rick Riordan is an exciting, action-packed book. But, it's only the beginning of Percy Jackson's story. I can't wait to read the rest of the books in the series to find out what happens next!

Book Review/Report • 149

WRITING MODELS AND FORMS

Minilesson 135

Understanding the Book Review

Objective: Understand the book review or report.

Guiding Question: How can I use these pages to help me write a good book review or report?

Teach/Model

Tell students to read the definition and bulleted points. Explain that the book report on these pages tells about *The Lightning Thief* by Rick Riordan. Then ask them to read to the end of p. 149.

Practice/Apply

Have students find the opinion in the conclusion of this book report. Ask *Does this book report make you want to read* The Lightning Thief?

Minilesson 136

Giving a Summary of a Book

Objective: Understand how to give a summary of a book.

Guiding Question: How do I give a summary of a book for my book report?

Teach/Model

Have students review Summary on pp. 106–107. Then explain that this book report briefly describes the main events, the setting, and the characters in *The Lightning Thief*. Point out that the summary tells only the most important parts of the book, using time order.

Practice/Apply

Using information in this book report, have students create a story map that identifies the main events, the setting, and the characters in *The Lightning Thief*.

Personal Narrative

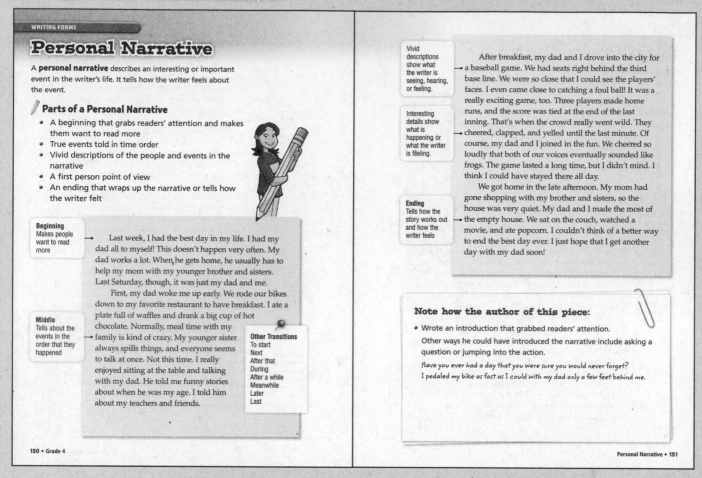

WRITING FORMS

Personal Narrative

A **personal narrative** describes an interesting or important event in the writer's life. It tells how the writer feels about the event.

Parts of a Personal Narrative

- A beginning that grabs readers' attention and makes them want to read more
- True events told in time order
- Vivid descriptions of the people and events in the narrative
- A first person point of view
- An ending that wraps up the narrative or tells how the writer felt

Beginning
Makes people want to read more

Last week, I had the best day in my life. I had my dad all to myself! This doesn't happen very often. My dad works a lot. When he gets home, he usually has to help my mom with my younger brother and sisters. Last Saturday, though, it was just my dad and me.

Middle
Tells about the events in the order that they happened

First, my dad woke me up early. We rode our bikes down to my favorite restaurant to have breakfast. I ate a plate full of waffles and drank a big cup of hot chocolate. Normally, meal time with my family is kind of crazy. My younger sister always spills things, and everyone seems to talk at once. Not this time. I really enjoyed sitting at the table and talking with my dad. He told me funny stories about when he was my age. I told him about my teachers and friends.

Other Transitions
To start
Next
After that
During
After a while
Meanwhile
Later
Last

Vivid descriptions show what the writer is seeing, hearing, or feeling.

After breakfast, my dad and I drove into the city for a baseball game. We had seats right behind the third base line. We were so close that I could see the players' faces. I even came close to catching a foul ball! It was a really exciting game, too. Three players made home runs, and the score was tied at the end of the last inning. That's when the crowd really went wild. They cheered, clapped, and yelled until the last minute. Of course, my dad and I joined in the fun. We cheered so loudly that both of our voices eventually sounded like frogs. The game lasted a long time, but I didn't mind. I think I could have stayed there all day.

Interesting details show what is happening or what the writer is feeling.

Ending Tells how the story works out and how the writer feels

We got home in the late afternoon. My mom had gone shopping with my brother and sisters, so the house was very quiet. My dad and I made the most of the empty house. We sat on the couch, watched a movie, and ate popcorn. I couldn't think of a better way to end the best day ever. I just hope that I get another day with my dad soon!

Note how the author of this piece:

- Wrote an introduction that grabbed readers' attention.

  Other ways he could have introduced the narrative include asking a question or jumping into the action.

  Have you ever had a day that you were sure you would never forget?
  I pedaled my bike as fast as I could with my dad only a few feet behind me.

150 • Grade 4

Personal Narrative • 151

Minilesson 137

Understanding the Personal Narrative

Objective: Understand the personal narrative.

Guiding Question: How can I use these pages to help me write a good personal narrative?

Teach/Model

Instruct students to read the definition and the bulleted points that follow it. Explain that the example on these pages is a personal narrative about a very enjoyable day the writer experienced. Then have students read to the end of p. 151.

Practice/Apply

Have students make a list of the vivid descriptions in this personal narrative that help them understand the people and events.

Minilesson 138

Using First-Person Point of View

Objective: Use first-person point of view in a personal narrative.

Guiding Question: From what point of view will I write my personal narrative?

Teach/Model

Explain to students that most personal narratives are written from the first-person point of view, or when the narrator who tells the story also takes part in the action. Point out the pronouns *I*, *my*, and *me* in the first paragraph of the personal narrative.

Practice/Apply

Have students write a paragraph about an enjoyable day they experienced. Remind them to use the first-person point of view.

Labels and Captions

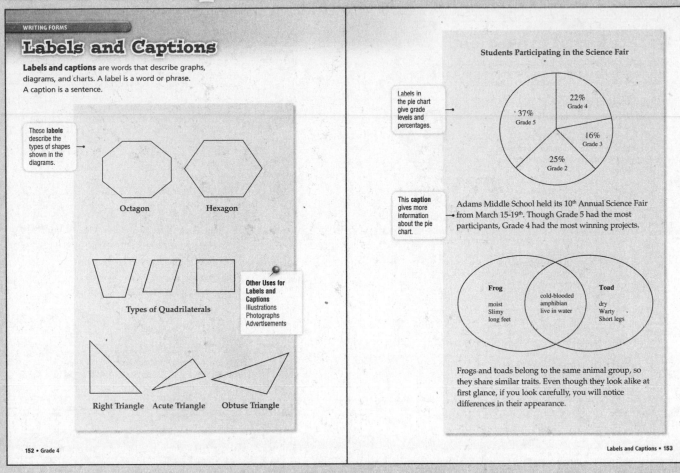

WRITING FORMS

Labels and Captions

Labels and captions are words that describe graphs, diagrams, and charts. A label is a word or phrase. A caption is a sentence.

These **labels** describe the types of shapes shown in the diagrams.

Octagon Hexagon

Types of Quadrilaterals

Other Uses for Labels and Captions
Illustrations
Photographs
Advertisements

Right Triangle Acute Triangle Obtuse Triangle

152 • Grade 4

Students Participating in the Science Fair

Labels in the pie chart give grade levels and percentages.

22% Grade 4
37% Grade 5
16% Grade 3
25% Grade 2

This **caption** gives more information about the pie chart.

Adams Middle School held its 10th Annual Science Fair from March 15-19th. Though Grade 5 had the most participants, Grade 4 had the most winning projects.

Frog
moist
Slimy
long feet

cold-blooded
amphibian
live in water

Toad
dry
Warty
Short legs

Frogs and toads belong to the same animal group, so they share similar traits. Even though they look alike at first glance, if you look carefully, you will notice differences in their appearance.

Labels and Captions • 153

WRITING MODELS AND FORMS

Minilesson 139

Understanding Labels

Objective: Understand the use of labels.

Guiding Question: How can I use these pages to help me write good labels for graphs, diagrams, and charts?

Teach/Model

Instruct students to read the definition on p. 152. Then explain that the labels on these pages help describe different kinds of graphs, diagrams, and charts. Tell students to closely examine labels on the graphic organizers on pp. 152–153.

Practice/Apply

Have students find examples of labels for graphic organizers in textbooks, magazines, or newspapers. Ask them to discuss what makes a good label.

Minilesson 140

Understanding Captions

Objective: Understand the use of captions.

Guiding Question: How can I use these pages to help me write good captions for graphs, diagrams, and charts?

Teach/Model

Tell students to read the two captions on p. 153. Point out that captions are written in sentences. Explain that captions are brief yet should be clear and accurate.

Practice/Apply

Provide students with a graph, diagram, or chart that does not have a caption but could include one to explain its ideas. Have them write a one- or two-sentence caption that gives information about the graphic organizer.

Notetaking Strategies

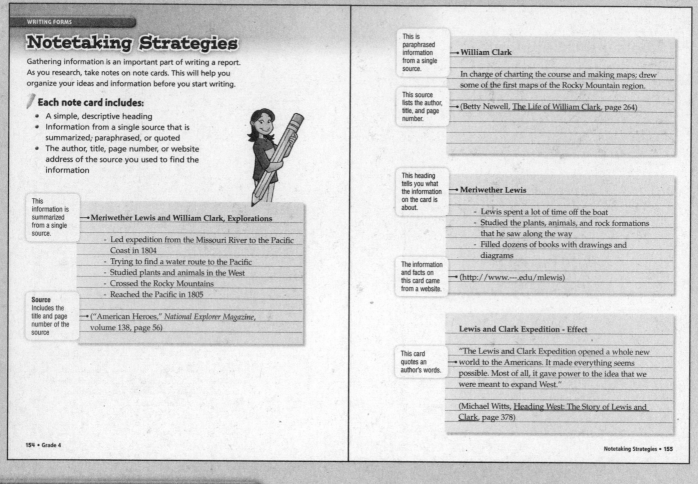

Notetaking Strategies

Gathering information is an important part of writing a report. As you research, take notes on note cards. This will help you organize your ideas and information before you start writing.

Each note card includes:

- A simple, descriptive heading
- Information from a single source that is summarized, paraphrased, or quoted
- The author, title, page number, or website address of the source you used to find the information

This information is summarized from a single source.

Meriwether Lewis and William Clark, Explorations

- Led expedition from the Missouri River to the Pacific Coast in 1804
- Trying to find a water route to the Pacific
- Studied plants and animals in the West
- Crossed the Rocky Mountains
- Reached the Pacific in 1805

Source Includes the title and page number of the source

("American Heroes," *National Explorer Magazine*, volume 138, page 56)

This is paraphrased information from a single source.

William Clark

In charge of charting the course and making maps; drew some of the first maps of the Rocky Mountain region.

This source lists the author, title, and page number.

(Betty Newell, *The Life of William Clark*, page 264)

This heading tells you what the information on the card is about.

Meriwether Lewis

- Lewis spent a lot of time off the boat
- Studied the plants, animals, and rock formations that he saw along the way
- Filled dozens of books with drawings and diagrams

The information and facts on this card came from a website.

(http://www.---.edu/mlewis)

This card quotes an author's words.

Lewis and Clark Expedition - Effect

"The Lewis and Clark Expedition opened a whole new world to the Americans. It made everything seems possible. Most of all, it gave power to the idea that we were meant to expand West."

(Michael Witts, *Heading West: The Story of Lewis and Clark*, page 378)

Minilesson 141

Using Note Cards

Objective: Understand how to take notes using note cards.

Guiding Question: How do I use these pages to help me make note cards for my report?

Teach/Model

Tell students to read the introduction and the bulleted points. Explain that the sample note cards on these pages show different ways to take notes about the explorers Meriwether Lewis and William Clark. Ask students to read to the end of p. 155.

Practice/Apply

Have students examine the sources that are listed on each note card. Have them discuss how information from magazines, books, and websites is cited.

Minilesson 142

Summarizing, Paraphrasing, and Quoting

Objective: Summarize, paraphrase, or quote information.

Guiding Question: How do I summarize, paraphrase, or quote information on my note cards?

Teach/Model

Point out that the first and third note cards summarize information, the second card restates information using different words, and the last card quotes an author.

Practice/Apply

Have students take notes on another explorer, such as Henry Hudson or Ponce de Leon. Ask them to make a series of note cards that summarize, paraphrase, and quote information from different sources.

Journal

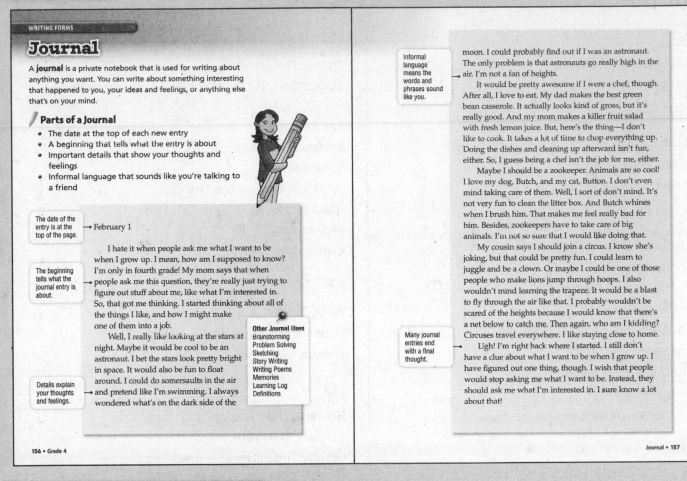

Minilesson 143

Understanding the Journal

Objective: Understand the journal.

Guiding Question: How can I use these pages to help write entries in a journal?

Teach/Model

Ask students to read the definition and bulleted points. Explain that the journal entry on these pages tells the writer's ideas and feelings about his or her interests. Then have students read to the end of p. 157.

Practice/Apply

Have students discuss the Other Journal Uses box on p. 156. Ask them to write a journal entry that fits one or more of these purposes.

Minilesson 144

Using Informal Language

Objective: Use informal language in a journal.

Guiding Question: What natural-sounding words and phrases should I use in my journal entries?

Teach/Model

Explain to students that this journal entry uses words and phrases that seem as if the writer is talking to a friend. For example, point out *awesome, gross,* and *here's the thing* in the third paragraph of the entry.

Practice/Apply

Have students find additional examples of informal language that the writer used in this journal entry. Have them discuss how these words and phrases reflect the writer's personality.

Index